ROLL WITH RAH

TALES OF AN UNDERGROUND DRIVER: VOLUME I

ROLL WITH RAH®

PUBLISHING AND PRODUCTIONS

RAHEIM WILSON

ROLL WITH RAH

TALES OF AN UNDERGROUND DRIVER: VOLUME I

Roll With Rah
Tales of an Underground Driver
Volume 1
by
Raheim Wilson

Library of Congress Contril Number: 1-11400182321
ISBN 979-8-9860774-0-6

Cover art by - Stevenson Estime
Photography by - Lamar Metcalf, 3E Creative Arts

Dedication

I would like to dedicate this book to the three most important women in my life. The first shout out goes to my biggest supporter from the moment she pushed me out of her womb. Thank you, Mother dear. You are the reason I was allowed to "find my way". If not for you, I hate to think where I would be. The second mention goes to the backbone of the family, AKA "the rock", my grandmother, Frances Shoffner. Unfortunately, granny passed away on Christmas Night, 2019, at the ripe old age of 97. Even on her death bed, she enabled me to find mistakes in my manuscript, as I read it to her. There is no doubt that her spirit is guiding me on this journey. The third mention goes to my only child Qianna Naimah Wilson. From birth you were the thing that gave my life purpose and direction. Knowing that you were depending on me has been the driving force behind all of my successes since the very beginning.

Of course, I can't end this dedication without acknowledging the countless folks, that have helped make Rollwithrah Publishing and Productions a reality. Y'all know who y'all are.

Finally, I had to save the best for last. A huge shout out and thank you goes to all of my passengers. Even the bad ones. Without all of you, there is no story to tell. To everyone reading this, buckle up, and enjoy the ride. Thank you for Rollin with Rah.

Table of Contents

Introduction

The weatherman was talking about it was going to rain. You know that those folks are wrong half the time. It didn't matter, I was at the local carwash. In my line of work, I'm expected to be shining regardless of the weather. The reflection of the sun was shimmering on my freshly waxed hood when my cell phone rang. I recognized the impatient, greeting-skipping, familiar rasp on the other end immediately. As usual he was telling me he needed to "bust a move." "It will take at least an hour to get to you bro," I answered. "Say no more," the voice blurted as he quickly hung up.

The beginning of summer was always an exciting time, especially in New York City. On this run, I was headed upstate to take a dude named Flako, to "see" somebody. Common verbiage means something completely different on the streets, so it's safe to assume whenever someone out here uses the word "see" in that manner, it means something fishy is going on. The word flako is Spanish for skinny, and this light-in-the-pants-ass drug dealer is going to "see" his customer, either to do a deal or settle some beef.

All those small towns looked alike to me, so I don't really remember what part of upstate New York we went to, and honestly it didn't matter because I was getting paid. Our journey finished in the driveway of a middle aged and recently widowed Caucasian woman. A few years prior, her husband blew his head off with a shotgun. On the two hour drive up, Flako told me the story of him helping her clean her late husband's brains off the bedroom sized walk-in closet wall. After hearing the story, I couldn't help but wonder how much she liked walking in the closet afterwards. The story was sad. The husband had a landscaping business which had fallen upon hard times. At his lowest point, weary and unable to further weather the storm, he decided to kill himself. Suicide is always tragic and painful for everyone. If he found solace, blessings to him. However, I believe that taking one's own life is the ultimate sin, and it certainly puts to rest chances of success in the next life.

I am going to share with you some things, which may seem hard to believe. As a driver, you see and hear the strangest things while meeting a host of people from all walks of life. The spectrum ranges from musicians and rappers to your everyday hustlers like Flako. Now don't get me wrong, there is nothing everyday about a hustler besides their dedication to the grind. Based on my time spent in the streets, I've learned successful hustlers are a rare breed. Success is objective, but to the streets, successful means they've avoided getting arrested, killed, or locked up. Typically, the word hustler is synonymous with drug dealer. However, my experiences have shown me that a hustler is anyone in society who is grinding hard to make a dollar. Everybody from the President of The United States to the local preacher is a hustler.

Street hustlers share similar traits with the rest of society. There are some of us out here who are virtuous, honest, humble, and hardworking. At the same time, you have people walking around that are deceitful, conniving, cutthroat and downright ruthless. My vehicle, Candy, has seen them all. During these late New York City nights, some of our best customers were strippers. Stripping isn't anything but another hustle. Despite what most of society may think, most strippers don't enjoy taking their clothes off and being fondled for a living. They're just trying to pay the bills like the other ninety-nine percent of the population, while there seems to be about one percent that has it all figured out.

This is the life I chose, or more accurately, the life that chose me . When people request a large unit, as a driver , you never know what you are getting yourself into. Maybe it's a bunch of rowdy teens looking to cause mayhem or maybe it's a family on the way to or from church. Every day in the business is completely different from the next.

I drive a 2002, Chevrolet, Z 71. Even though it's the sport version of the popular Chevy Suburban, it's still a big unit. There was a time when Candy and I had the pleasure of transporting, ten smoking-hot Latina beauties to a nightclub in Manhattan. Not only were they gorgeous, but they also tipped well. Like most passengers, we connected with them through an underground cab base. It wasn't like a secret lair or anything. The building was definitely on the street, but it was an underground base because they weren't registered with the New York City Taxi Limousine Commission (TLC).

My car service is called Roll with Rah. I am Rah, it's short for Raheim. I am the sole owner and driver for now, but something tells me not for long. There is a lot of money to be made in this business if you have the right attitude and approach. My unit number is 99. The taxi radio under the driver's seat is the lifeline to the base. Driving for an underground base means waiting, sometimes for hours for a voice to come through the speaker with a location and party size. That is known as "first shout." If a driver decides to squeeze their microphone (key up) to respond, they are agreeing to be at the pick-up location in five minutes or less. Some of the more popular bases' "first shout" is three minutes. If two drivers key up at the same time, the one with the stronger signal will get to the base first. One day, a livery cab driver told me his "first shout" was one minute on his base. I couldn't imagine having to be at a destination for a pick-up in one minute. It's no wonder that half of the cabs in this city drive so recklessly.

When, "second shout" comes from the dispatcher (B-1) they repeat the location, along with the number of people in the party (ex. 2 males, 1 child) and the location they are going to. "Second shout" was 10 minutes or less and then the "third shout" from the base on a call is open time. "Open time" means just what it sounds like ; they'll get there whenever. I was always surprised how long people were willing to wait for a particular unit to come and pick them up. Then again if the unit has the amenities that you are looking for, be it TV's, video games, or a nice stereo system, I can understand them waiting. There was a point in time when I was driving my fares around, envious of them because of the beautiful simplicity of being a passenger. You get to drink, smoke, eat and ride, while listening to the latest tunes and people-watching as you glide through the most famous city on earth. I was sometimes envious of the luxury provided for my passengers. I was working so hard, it would have been nice for somebody to drive me around, for once.

Introduction

My time spent in the streets have taken me through some of the grittiest neighborhoods in the country. "Stay on point," was a common phrase we would say to each other. The origin of the phrase was military, and we didn't know how fitting it was—considering the war zones we traversed through for routine errands. The streets don't have any picks, and these blocks will chew you up and spit you out faster than you can react. Not everyone that you pick up will have good intentions but lucky for me, I have never had anyone attempt to assault or rob me. In fact, the only individuals to ever approach me in a threatening manner were members of the biggest gang in New York--the NYPD. People all over the world call the cops all types of things unique to the locale, 'Book 'em Jake,' 'Teddy,' 'Five O,' 'The Fuzz,' 'the boys'.… It all means the same thing. While the scenarios always change, the one thing that remains constant is that as a Black man, at some point, I am almost definitely going to be harassed by the police. Baffling really, that I've unknowingly driven murderers safely to their destination without any fear for my life, only to feel my adrenaline surge while being targeted picking up chicken, by the same people hired to protect and serve.

That trip upstate, for the widow of the husband who blew his brains out and the wife had to clean them up with Flako, was on May 20, 2004. I used to keep a record of all the significant and high-earning trips on the calendar. Over time, the trips became so frequent, I abandoned the idea. I was paid $300 for that two-hour drive. Three hundred dollars would become a good starting point for negotiating out- of-town runs. If asked, I would say it's a decent way to make a living considering the money earned so far, has been enough to sustain me. Truthfully, it's still not enough and probably never will be, but I'm grateful to be able to stay afloat and even swim at times.

Sometimes, I used to sleep in my truck and wait for the B-1 to spit something good over the radio. Staying in the car gave an added advantage. When a call came in, the only thing that had to be done was turn the key and go. As a matter of fact, I have met some of my best passengers at what we like to call the "creep hours," the time of night people are creeping around under the cover of darkness. Obviously, rendezvous and shady deals take place all the time, but they're much more prevalent during those hours. Imagine you needed a car at 3:30 AM in the middle of the winter. Most people were tucked in their beds, but Rah was out there, waiting. There was always heavy competition for the good calls that came out during peak times, but my niche was grabbing the crumbs. Ten and twenty-five dollars here and there may not sound like a lot, but it all adds up to bills being paid along with connections being made.

Flako and his custie (short for customer) had been dealing with one another for seven years. When a customer is faithful and has paid you so much over time, a real bond develops. I understood because I had custies that I had developed genuine love for, and there was no distance you won't travel for someone that has been holding you down. That trip upstate with Flako allowed me to take the rest of the night off, so I watched the Nets get knocked out of the playoffs by the Detroit Pistons with my mom, grandma, and daughter.

When it is time for me to lay my head to rest, it's usually at granny's placc in Harlem. I feel like everybody's heard of

Harlem. Harlem is located in the upper west part of Manhattan. It starts at 110th Street, just north of Central Park and runs up to approximately 155th Street. East to west, it stretches from 5th Avenue over to Morningside Avenue. East of 5th Avenue is considered Spanish Harlem, which is where I grew up…well, that's where we lived after my mother moved us to the Eastside from the real Harlem. My first few years of life were spent on 149th Street between 7th and 8th Avenues. Granny's apartment is now located a few blocks away, over on 5th Avenue, and within walking distance. If I was not at Granny's, I was in the streets. The main purpose of me being in New York was to make money, not to sleep, so I still keep an overnight bag with clothes in it in the back of the truck. Whenever the work was done, I would leave New York and head home to the mountains without having to stop and pack. Being able to bounce out of town at a moment's notice came in handy. If I stay ready, I never have to get ready.

It's fascinating the number of things you can learn and places you can see when out, dealing with public. As a driver, I got to observe the way a man treats his woman and how mothers parent their children. I saw how different cliques interact with one another. There is always a hierarchy in any group setting. Some things you must see to believe, and that is the only reason I know some of the stories from the decade plus are real.

There was this one call that originated at the Throgs Neck Housing Projects. A guy called the cab base for a large unit so that he could go shopping for a Father's Day BBQ that he was hosting. The dude and his girlfriend were heading to a meat market in Queens. The round trip would be worth at least eighty dollars for me, and by the time it was done, he had done close to $600 worth of shopping. After arriving back at the projects, he paid me $100 for the round trip with a one-hundred-dollar bill. The entire mission took less than two hours, and to show appreciation, I offered to help him upstairs with the bags. When I entered his crib, I was shocked at the disarray which laid before my eyes.

There was a petite brown skinned chick that looked to be in her mid-20's. A little tike, barely one years old, in a walker toddled along behind her deftly weaving through the clothes and random bullshit scattered about the house. The kitchen sink and counter were overflowing with dirty dishes and left little space to place any bags. He told me just to drop them on the floor and come on in the room. Some people's first instinct is to put meat from the store in the refrigerator, and others, not so much. Glancing towards the tattered and soiled furniture in the living room, I wondered how long it had been around. How hard would it have been for him to just go to a Rent-A-Center and rent to own some decent furniture?

I had to go to the bathroom and obviously, that was messy too. I went, and walked back to the living room, which needed a different title based on its condition, when the smell of marijuana hit me before I could even reach the area. As the kid rolled around, everyone was sitting around smiling and laughing like everything was normal. I recognize people having different standards of living, and to this family I'm sure this was the norm, but none of it was cool with me. I liked to smoke every now and again, but I tried to avoid doing so around children. In this instance, I was the driver and not there to preach a sermon, so like all of the rest of the nonsense I had noticed since walking through the door, I ignored it.

Since it seemed like I would be here for more than a few minutes, I found a chair to sit on that didn't look too shady. After a while, I noticed that the dude and his girl had slid off somewhere. Once the blunts were done, I was pretty much ready to go too. While poking my head into one of the rear rooms to say my goodbyes, I found them, much to my surprise laying fully clothed on two twin mattresses stacked on top of one another. I shook my head, while thinking, they didn't even have an adult-sized bed for themselves.

Walking me to the door, the dude invited me to come to the BBQ. "Unfortunately, I can't…" I said, "My plan was to be spending Father's Day in Pennsylvania with my family." Even if I had nowhere in particular to be on Father's Day, one thing is for sure, I would not have been caught dead eating a bit of food at any BBQ they were responsible for. Even if they're grilling, the food must be prepped somewhere and based on the despicable condition of the house, I wouldn't trust it.

As it turned out, everything I did that day was for free. The one-hundred-dollar bill used as payment was one of the older ones. In 2003, the currency in the US was redesigned and the small pictures on the paper notes were replaced with a big face. Additionally, other security features were added to the bills, like tamper-proof paper and watermarks. For some reason, later that evening when looking at the hundred-dollar bill I received, it didn't feel real. I had gotten so used to the big-faced money that my mind didn't remember what a small-faced hundred-dollar bill looked and felt like.

Clearly that dude was into all types of stuff. I started thinking that counterfeit money might be one of his hustles. My brother used to get his hands on "funny money" and bust em down, so I figured he would have been the man to go and see. Either way, I knew my mind or maybe my sub-conscience was playing tricks on me because I knew better than to be in that house smoking around kids and chilling with people I really didn't want to be socializing with. I used them for the free weed after getting $100 for an easy job, and karma is a funny thing sometimes. Something made me tear up the money into shreds and toss it out of my sunroof, towards the end of the night. In hindsight, that was fucking stupid because worst case scenario, even if it was a fake, I could have passed it off to someone else.

Some fools put a set of twenty-thousand-dollar rims on their car but still live home with their mother. That reminds me of a story I heard about a guy I knew named, Bebo. As the story goes, the kid owned a 2000 Cadillac Escalade which was easily a fifty-thousand-dollar vehicle. To get to his bedroom, he had to cut through his mother's bedroom in one of those old railroad style apartments. So essentially, he had to walk his guests of the opposite sex past his mother. He clearly wasn't focused on saving that money and had his priorities wrong. Decision-making is a critical life skill. If given a logical choice, it is my assumption that most people will make sound and logical decisions. Then again, you never can be too sure.

Sometimes the good choices are spelled out clearly, yet people still make poor decisions.

As an "OJ," we charged between thirty and fifty dollars an hour. Before we go any further, let's break down what "OJ" means. Ghetto legend has it that there was a man nicknamed OJ back in the mid-1980s. As was the case in many ghettoes across the country drugs were running rampant in New York City. With the influx of drugs, there was suddenly a tremendous amount of money in the streets and a lot of product being moved around. OJ came up with the idea of using regular cars to move around to avoid the unwanted attention that riding in regular looking taxis would attract. From that point on, underground drivers were known as OJs.

These days, fifty to sixty dollars an hour isn't bad and if the call was a special one, say a prom, funeral or wedding, the fee would go up accordingly. For the most part, my passengers could afford the somewhat steep prices. Either they have put money aside because they knew they were going out, or because they were just getting money like that and spending a couple of dollars wouldn't hurt their pockets in the least. Most of them were in the street life one way or the other and they ran scams, sold drugs, robbed, stole, pimped, stripped, etc., and they all wanted to travel in style. I tried to build a different relationship with each regular. As a driver, you need your regulars because they're consistent cash. For them, it's a blessing for to have a driver they can trust. Especially when you are hustling illegally, you don't want random drivers. It's a terrible idea to have a bunch of people knowing what you're doing.

A gypsy cab is normally a Lincoln Town Car instead of the yellow or green livery cabs. The color varies from city to city. When moving around illegally, one wants to blend in as much as possible . Standing out, in a marked ride is just as good as painting a cop's bullseye on your head. Having TLC plates (taxi license plates) lets everybody know it's a cab. These days they even have a sticker on the passenger window of the taxicab, which states, "You are being videotaped for your own and for the driver's safety." That same sticker goes on to say, "This vehicle may be stopped and searched at any time by the police for the driver's safety." In full transparency, there have been many incidents where cab drivers were robbed and sometimes killed. However, in a post-crack era NYC, I know they were not stopping cars to check on anyone's safety. They are profiling, looking for an excuse to pull the car over and arrest someone. If a driver is driving with a suspended driver's license, he will be arrested. If they can't arrest the driver for something, then they'll start questioning the passenger. At one point, my license was suspended because of failure to pay a ticket for a seatbelt violation. The police stopped me for some random reason; I was arrested and thrown in the same jail cell with the real criminals. I was fingerprinted and had my picture taken and had to go in front of a judge and everything.

I know it's important for all drivers to be properly licensed and insured, but does the guy with a seatbelt ticket need to go to jail, let alone be placed in a cell alongside the dude that had a bar fight and beat up five people? I don't think so. The cops grease the wheels of the system by keeping a lot of people like judges, corrections officers, and clerks employed. It's exactly like an officer randomly walking up to you on the street and questioning you without probable cause, which is usually illegal, but under "Stop and Frisk" laws, such stops were deemed acceptable. Needless-to-say, this is an inconvenience and a waste of time that your average person would much rather avoid. By riding in an unmarked vehicle you tremendously increase your chances of safe passage. Additionally, when you call an OJ, it's a completely different riding experience.

Most of the vehicles driven by members of the underground base are commonly referred to as "fly rides." Rap legend, Nas, once called them "system jeeps" in his song "Street Dreams." However, he was not entirely accurate in his depiction because all units are not jeeps. When someone calls a base to get an OJ, they may be picked up by a Lexus, Cadillac, Mercedes-Benz, BMW or whatever. Unless you request a certain vehicle you never know what will come, and every unit isn't a luxury car. Remember, what starts out as a top-of-the-line vehicle is not as trendy as it was five years prior. A few years on these New York City streets will age any vehicle . Honestly, between all the potholes and the reckless drivers, you are fortunate to still have your vehicle on the road after five years. Most drivers don't even last that long.

Alex was a chubby Spanish kid and about nineteen at the time that I met him. He lived on Clay Avenue in The Bronx and started out as a passenger of mine. About three or four years after we first met, he came to me one day and said, "Instead of being a cash paying customer, I'm ready to become a money-making driver." Alex started out with a regular car and shortly after upgraded his vehicle to a brand-new Hummer.

The Hummer is a luxury SUV, designed to pretty much mirror the military version, sans the machine gun turret on the top. Although, I wouldn't be surprised if some millionaire had their Hummer outfitted with one because that's something I could see myself doing if I had the resources. Manufactured by the GMC and retailing for about sixty-thousand-dollars, the monthly car note must have been at least $750. His truck had televisions and an amazing stereo system to the point when he turned it all the way up, it was heard from three blocks away. I'm sure that probably earned him a few noise-pollution tickets.

After several years, I stopped working with the cab base and decided to go on my own. I was curious to know how things were going with the boys on the base, so I checked back with Alex. Surprisingly, Alex told me that he was no longer in the business, and he had taken a job as a security guard. The sadness in his tone was unforgettable, especially when he actually said, "I'm not a driver anymore," out loud. He had lasted maybe a year, two years at the max. He didn't say anything at the time, but something pretty horrible must have happened to force him out of something that he was heavily invested in. I never asked Alex why he wasn't in the business anymore. There was no need to open up old wounds.

While transporting hundreds of people around, it's only a matter of time before some things will spill, get burned, chipped, defaced or whatever. Nonetheless, a five-year-old Suburban still looks better than a majority of the livery cabs that can be seen cruising through your local neighborhood. If you get a chance, next time you are in NYC, pay attention to the condition of some of the cabs around you. You're guaranteed to at least hear brakes screeching. An OJ typically is in better overall condition because unlike a regular cab, OJs are personal vehicles just being used part time for a cab service. Chances are that the owner takes the time to keep his vehicle up to par. Again, these vehicles are often equipped with several different amenities and mine was no different. I had a small seven-inch screen in the front which was connected to a Sony PlayStation located under the passenger seat. However, amenities attract attention and consequently, that TV was stolen. The worst part was it didn't even happen overnight. The theft happened at approximately 6 PM in front of my aunt's building in The Bronx. They obviously were amateurs since they didn't even check for the PlayStation.

Criminal activity is not the only reason that a person would want to call an OJ. Everyone wants to arrive in style, and the luxury of an OJ is a very appealing aspect; but the convenience is the biggest selling point. When you are with an OJ, you can make three or four stops and just pay the rate for one hour. The cost to rent a regular car is $30 an hour. Think about how much time and money would be wasted trying to go from cab to cab to cab while you run your errands. At least an OJ waits for you as you run around.

Again, that is the importance of regulars. If you know who you are going to pick up, it practically eliminates the possibility of getting caught by the TLC. Getting caught by the TLC means a potential fine upwards of $800 and vehicle confiscation. Granted, most regulars start as strangers, and eventually become regulars. Once they do, it's basically getting paid to ride around with your friends. There are passengers that have been "Rolling with Rah" since its inception in the summer of 2002. July 5, 2002 is the exact date that my life changed forever. Foe was one of my first regulars.

There are quite a few major highways running throughout NYC. Some are even the same road with a different name. It doesn't matter which route is taken, typically any major highway suffices. Some people are afraid of highways but for an OJ, it's a lot safer to be cruising the highway smoking instead of being in stop and go traffic where a random police car might pull up at any moment.

When the regulars step into Candy for the first time it's like they are falling in love. She's named Candy because once you get a taste of her, you want more and more. Brand new, riding in Candy, was as smooth as floating on air. The key to a person becoming a regular is the link between driver and passenger. As in any friendship or relationship, chemistry is essential; and a successful driver-passenger relationship is no different. To be a successful OJ, you have to be a people person, the same as any other customer service job. A passenger needs a positive and one-of-a-kind experience to want to call you back the next time they have to go anywhere. There are a plenty of car services that can have any random person at their doorstep in less than two minutes, so if they are willing to wait fifteen or twenty minutes for me, there's a reason.

That call back doesn't happen unless they like the unit, but mostly the driver. There are a lot of "Big Boy Trucks" on the block, but what separated me from the rest was my gift of gab. Some might say I inherited it from my father, Andrew James Wilson, who died on April 28, 2004 . This gift has been my most valuable asset. I have always gotten along with and been exposed to many different cultures and ethnicities, and the commonality is always the ability to communicate effectively. Biologically, we are all people with the same basic wants and needs. As long as you keep that in mind, you are able to deal with anyone you come in contact with.

Having regular passengers is also extra important because even though New York is known as the city that never sleeps, there are times when people simply aren't calling the base for a ride. It's a beautiful thing when you are just sitting around in your vehicle listening out for a call and then bling-bling, the telephone rings and whoever is on the other end of the phone looking to drop fifty to sixty dollars in your pocket. At a minimum, if a driver only managed to scrape a few calls from the base, they wind up earning at least $100 cash for the day, on a weekday. Weekends were a completely different story. On Friday and Saturday, a driver is looking at making $200 or more at least. The most money I ever made in one day was $380, I think, or maybe $400 and that was without leaving NYC. Out-of-town trips are a completely different situation.

Most of my business came from my cell phone. Even though I was facilitating my own rides, I still made it a point to pay my $70 base fee every week. If I was going out of town or didn't want to work, it would be as simple as not paying the base fee. The owner of my base, Duke, and I had a good working relationship. Base fee was due on Thursday, and that didn't sit well with me because I had moved to The Poconos and was caring for my daughter. I wasn't able to get back to New York until Thursday and wasn't about to go into my personal money for the base fee. Rule number 1, once money comes in the house it gets put aside for bills and is not to be touched if at all avoidable. The base fee, my snack money, and whatever else came straight from the streets on that particular day. Duke understood my plight and allowed me an extra day to pay. Sometimes I asked Duke, "Why do you collect before the weekend when you know sometimes the weekdays are slow?" His reply was "I have to get my money first."

Believe it or not, there are drivers that would work on the weekend and make their four or five hundred dollars and then simply not pay come Sunday if they were given the chance. By collecting before the weekend, it planted a seed of hunger inside of the driver to earn the money back that they had just put out. It all makes perfect sense in retrospect. Duke didn't have to understand my special circumstances, and I was appreciative of that. I'm sure if I was less of a people-person, he wouldn't have been as accommodating.

Being a driver is a job. To do ones' job properly, they must have the right tools. In order to be a successful OJ you need: 1. A nice ride, 2. People skills, and 3. A reliable phone. Few things make a worse impression than calling someone only to find that their phone has been temporarily disconnected. The next time you need a ride, you are not going to think of that person. How can a business phone be out of service?

As a driver it's helpful that you know how to navigate around the city that you are working in. Please keep in mind, the majority of this story took place prior to the world of GPS, which meant having a sense of direction and knowing how to navigate a map was the fourth essential tool for being an

OJ. Some people, for whatever reason, have difficulties doing those four things. It's more to it than that but covering those four bases will get a person off to a good start in their career as an OJ. I used to always say all I need is an address in New York City, and I will find my way there. From time to time, you would hear drivers getting directions from the B-1 over the radio. Back at the base, the B-1 would be looking it up on the map for them. That shit was crazy.

I was a 31-year-old grown man with grown folk's bills. It wasn't a game for me. I surveyed the terrain, analyzed what would be needed to succeed and attacked with absolute faith in God. I was a man trying to take care of his family. Depending on how you look at it, because of my professional background, I was accustomed to a certain lifestyle. If this is what I had to master in order for us to continue to exist in the lifestyle we had become used to, then so be it.

Your level of success is directly connected to the amount of work that a person is prepared to invest. I've had an office job. At 21, I started working at a construction company as the messenger, which also turned out to be the copy and fax machine maintenance man. About three years later, I climbed my way out of that position to the role of Inspector. The company outfitted me with a '96 Ford Taurus which I kept 24 hours a day for approximately 18 months; all expenses paid, including my cell phone bill. I always managed to run out of gas on Friday and need to refill on a Monday or Tuesday. Eventually I became an assistant Project Manager in that same company, specializing in interior renovations. Whether it was the corporate world or the underworld, the same rules apply.

It's all about how you carry yourself in any given situation. It doesn't matter what the position is, the goal is to be the best. How you handle your business is what people see and respect. I can't believe that it will be almost twenty years come July 5, 2022 since Roll with Rah has been off the ground. It seems like only yesterday.

Chapter 1:
The Origin

I mentioned that I have been in this line of work since July 2002, but that's not entirely accurate. Back in 1999, I was laid-off from my first construction job. Employment fluctuates like a rollercoaster and when the jobs are on the downward slope, the layoffs are close behind. At the time, I was single, with plenty of bills and raising a three-year-old daughter by myself. In addition to rent for our apartment on the Eastside of Manhattan, as I'm sure most parents would agree about their own children—my daughter, Qianna, was expensive without me paying for anything outside of the necessities. Back then I drove a blue '98 Ford Expedition named Tigger, which I named directly inspired by Winnie the Pooh's Tiger companion. The name was fitting because, like a Tiger, Tigger attacked the road with the aggressive roar of her engine.

I remember sitting parked in Tigger, in my old neighborhood visibly uncomfortable and distraught when my homeboy, Los, walked up and asked why I was looking so "bummed out." After all, it was a beautiful June day, complete with all the fixings of a New York City summer, sans the raincloud that was my layoff hovering above me. After hearing what happened, Los said to me while pointing to my truck, "Don't worry, you got this." I now this fool ain't thinking I'm about to sell my fucking truck, so I asked him, "What do you mean Los?" He told me about the base where he was a driver. At the time, I had no idea what he was talking about. I had no memory of Los ever driving a taxicab. He went on to explain how the base worked and told me that I could make a lot of cash because I had a "big boy V." My favorite Socrates quote is, "I know that I know nothing." I knew I was from Harlem, and thought I knew what was going on in the streets. I knew, up until very recently, I had a legal job and my own truck. I knew I had no reason to deal with bases because I seldom needed a ride. What I didn't know, was the journey this talk was going to send me on.

I lived in Spanish Harlem, so learning a new borough would be a challenge. I would be forced to learn this hustle from the ground up. That is exactly how it should be. There are no shortcuts to success. Los told me there was nothing to worry about. Ya kinda lied about that part homie. But it's all good. We made plans to go uptown the next day to get me started. Later that night, I mulled over the decision I just made. The answer was not clear, what was crystal clear was the amount printed on my bills every month.

The next day I picked Los up from in front of our building, and we headed to a barbershop at the intersection of Watson and White Plains Avenues in The Bronx. It was about one block away from the Bruckner Expressway, and easy to find. As we were pulling up, I asked, "I brought you to get a haircut?" "No Rah, the base is in the back of the barbershop," he chuckled. "Remember this is an underground base, so it's not like they could hang a bright neon sign that says, 'Car Service.'"

The owner of the base, Duke, was out so we had to hang around for about an hour. When he got back, Los made a brief intro, then explained my situation. Of course, Duke had no problem with me joining the base, it meant more money for him in terms of base fee and repeater fee. For Duke's base, each driver is worth approximately $300 a month. The Base Fee was $70 a week and the repeater fee was $30 a month. All of this was another language, so I asked Duke, what the repeater fee was. He went on to explain a repeater is a piece of equipment which allows the calls to be broadcasted for drivers to hear, and the bill had to be paid every month, just like a phone bill.

After squaring things with Duke, Los took me to the radio shop so I could get connected. The whole time while waiting for the installation, I was secretly beaming with excitement thinking about the new chapter I was embarking on. Raheim Wilson, "The 9-to-5 Working Man" was slowly dying with every screw drilled and wire soldered. My unit number was 100, pronounced one hundred, but that is not how the B-1 and other drivers were going to speak it. One-Double Oh or just plain One-Double was the right way to say it, and he was on the scene and ready to get this money.

My spirit was in the right place, and still had no idea how cabbing actually worked. So, in the spirit of true friendship, Los volunteered to ride "double" with me. Riding double means there are two people in the unit. Most bases only allow a male and female to ride double, but an exception was made so my boy could school me real quick. Could you imagine the unease a young woman might feel getting into a strange vehicle with not one, but two men she's never seen before ? Regardless, my arrangement with Los came at a premium. Los agreed to show me the ropes and asked in turn I give him half of whatever I earned. All business is about leverage and exchange, and that sounded fair enough to me considering that without Los, I would be home throwing a one-man pity party or hopping from temp agency to temp agency begging for work.

The first day was the next day, and after waiting on the side of the road for over an hour and growing increasingly more restless, I turned to Los and asked, "Is this all we do? Why can't we just pick up any one of these people that we passed standing there with their hand out trying to hail a cab?" That's when Los explained the laws and why that was strictly forbidden because we weren't licensed. He summed up his rant with, "If the wrong person were to see that, there would be hell to pay." Besides if your passenger were intent on mischief and god forbid the police got involved, you would have a record of them calling the base for a ride as part of your defense.

After some time, we finally got our first call. The pickup was an older man, in his mid to late fifties making two stops in The Bronx. The term OJs used to define more than one stop is, "Slight" and it's short for slight hold. The rate for a slight is $20 per 30 minutes. B-1 told him we were riding double; he accepted the ride, and we were on our way to get him. The call went smoothly. He was a cool guy and didn't say much. After making his rounds, we arrived back at his place, and before he exited the vehicle, he looked at Los and I with a smile and said, "Ok now…y'all youngsters be safe out here in these streets." We made about $30 each over the next couple of hours, nothing to race to the bank about. Then suddenly, as if divine timing couldn't be any more divine, the B-1 threw out a timed pick up for six females. I sat frozen, almost shell-shocked and in disbelief when the call came out. Los being the savvy vet he was, immediately snatched the microphone from my lap and keyed up like his life depended on it. We got the call.

The call was a 7 PM pickup for six women. They were going to The Meadowlands at Giants Stadium for the Summer Jam concert. Summer Jam is a huge annual production sponsored by the local radio station, Hot 97. As expected, the concert always includes some of the most popular Rap and R&B artists and draws a very large crowd. The fee to go to the Meadowlands from The Bronx was $80, $40 of which had to go to Los. Fortunately, the call was a round trip because a trip to the Meadowlands on public transportation takes over two hours. After dropping the ladies off, we shot back to the city to catch a few more calls. I was finally comfortable and, in a groove, when it was time to get the women from the concert. I turned to my right and said, "I got this. I don't need you to escort me Bro. Also, I wanted the whole pick up fee for the return trip to myself." Los understood and asked me to drop him at his vehicle so that he could get to work.

One of my first regular passengers was a guy I grew up with named, DJ Darrell whose moniker was, Deezo. Deezo worked at one of the local strip clubs in Hunts Point called the Wedge Hall. My work night began everyday by taking Deezo to work at 8 PM. His rationale was if he is going to take a cab to and from work every day anyway, why wouldn't he just pay his boy? I certainly wasn't arguing with him on that. I'm a firm believer in paying my friends for their services, especially if they do good work. Most of that summer was spent in The Bronx. With my base in The Bronx, it only made sense for me to stay close to the money. After driving around all day, my nights ended with me picking up Deezo after the club closed at 4 AM. During those days, I typically made between $800 and $1,000 a week. It was the summertime, and the hood was full of people on the move going here and there.

That first tour as an OJ, back in '98 didn't offer any allusions of excitement, and there weren't many memories to recall. Although, there was one time, it was supposed to be a quick trip that I took upstate one summer evening. After Los stopped riding double with me, I muddled around trying to find my footing. As a rookie, I would snatch up anything I could. I was sitting in my unit around 1 AM when I heard the dispatcher call for a single male, slight hold, and I jumped on it. Back then I could barely understand the dispatchers when they spoke due to how fast they were speaking during the shouts; so, any call that I could understand and get to in a reasonable amount of time was good enough for me to jump on. The guy was being picked up from the housing projects on 144thStreet and 3rd Avenue. When I pulled up to the spot, there was a Spanish guy in his mid-to-late twenties waiting for me.

Before I could part my lips to greet him, he began speaking, "I haven't gotten in your truck yet." Outside of stating the obvious, his point was to set the expectation that there wouldn't be a money exchange if I didn't take him anywhere. Some drivers were known to extort the passenger for taking the call and arriving to pick the passenger up, even if they didn't actually take them to a destination. "I am going to Spring Valley, NY. How much is that?"

According to the book of fares the base handed out to all of us drivers, I was supposed to charge him almost a $100 to go to

Spring Valley. It was a little over forty minutes away from the city, and ironic enough, I used to drive up there every couple of weeks in the early 90's when my mom lived in " The Valley". That being said, I told him I'd only charge him $50 dollars. Incredulously, with his mouth open in disbelief he blurted, "Fifty dollars for the whole ride?" "Yeah, I know where it is," I replied smoothly.

With a smile, he climbed in Tigger and we were off. At that time of night, there was hardly any traffic, so we got there in less than half an hour. Having taken the drive so many times, I was on autopilot coming off the exit. Instinctively, I wanted to turn right as I had done so many times in the years prior. "Turn left up here," my co-pilot said. So, instead of taking a right like muscle memory insisted, I turned left. After driving about five minutes, we pulled upon what looked like a rundown housing development. All those years I spent driving to and from" The Valley' , I didn't even know that they had projects. Truthfully, I had been coming up there for five years and never once driven through that part of town. As he was about to get out, he tapped his pockets. "Shit!" he exclaimed between his teeth. I didn't know what was happening when he finally looked at me and said disappointingly, "I forgot to ask you to stop by the store. I needed to pick up some Dutches (Dutch master Cigars are one of the things used for rolling weed).

Spring Valley is the suburbs, so that meant unlike the in the hood, they don't have stores on every other corner, and that also meant adding an extra $25 to the tab. My real takeaway from the trip had nothing to do with financial gain. That was the introductory lesson to a theme I would see repeated as

I travelled all over the country. Everywhere has a ghetto. A place where society has managed to carve out a section of even the smallest towns and subjugate Black and Brown people to substandard conditions. It happens everywhere, and coded language allows us to believe the "hood" has managed to infiltrate what used to be a small, serene community like Spring Valley.

There is one dude from that first OJ tour that I still remember vividly even though it has been over two decades. The passenger was from the block of 146th Street between Brook and Willis Avenues in the South Bronx. This neighborhood is a blend of an old neighborhood dying and new one being born. On this block, construction had just finished on a series of attached houses. All the homes have freshly planted trees and a community mailbox in the middle of the block. While all of this seemed lovely enough, the picture is spoiled by adjacent housing projects and tenement buildings which undoubtedly are bustling with all sorts of criminal activity. I can't really blame my brothers and sisters in the projects. Equitable treatment, education and resources is a fundamental component of societal mobility. Left to our own devices, we've seen desperate people do sometimes incredible, and sometimes terrible things. The typical unemployed American will look for work, and work is what you make it. Back then, there was still plenty of drug money in the streets, so people made it. NYC, now and in the foreseeable future, will not be what it was; as most of these neighborhoods have been completely gentrified, and drugs aren't running rampant like they were.

The guy wasn't a drug dealer or anything like that. When we met, he was about twenty-one years old and spoke with a slight Jamaican accent. He stood about six feet tall and was always smiling big white teeth. His presence is hard to forget. I met him through the base, no surprise there. He had a large presence, one that would stay with you as it stayed with me. However, his name did not, so I am going to call him Jolly. Every time Jolly called me, he was going shopping or going to hang out with some girl, sometimes both. One afternoon, as we headed from Harlem across the 145th Street bridge, Jolly was telling me a story about what happened the night before. Our senses are strong, and anything can trigger a flashback. For Jolly, it was the song being played on the radio that caused Jolly to nearly jump out of his seat reliving the events in his mind. Excited, Jolly began jumping back and forth between English and Patois, "Mi brudda!…In de club last night, dem gals dem go crazy when dis song come on!" The song was, "Everyone Falls in Love Sometimes" by Tanto Metro and Devonte, and I can see why the ladies went crazy. The vibe was perfect for any party. I'm sure Jolly had a blast; I probably would have too.

Even though he wasn't a drug dealer, he was still connected to the trade. His mother was a "Queenpin." She controlled most of the weed and narcotics that flowed through her block, 146th Street. I never met her, so everything I learned about her came directly from Jolly. One thing he never shared was how she became head honcho. He told me that when he was eighteen, she rented out an empty store front and turned it into a game room for him to manage. Jolly had put a pool table in place and some tables and chairs on the side just in case anyone wanted to play some cards or dominoes. It was labeled as a social club, and basically it was a place for Jolly and his friends on the block to hang out without being harassed by the police. I am sure that more than one or two deals went down inside of those walls.

One day when I was dropping Jolly off, I decided to go inside the social club and hang out for a bit. I always kept a chessboard in the truck so whenever the topic came up, I could pull it out. There were plenty of brothers in the room that had been to jail, and Chess is one of the main ways to pass the time while locked up. Based on my relationship with the dude that ran the place, I automatically had the respect of everyone in the room. I had a great day chilling with Jolly and his boys, smoking weed and talking shit as we played Chess. Jolly's mom's plan was for him to inherit her hierarchy and business from her. He had studied her closely as he grew into manhood and was already taking steps in that direction. Everyone in the social club wasn't there to socialize, people knew who Jolly was and who he was destined to become. There's nothing glorious about the drug game, it's a dirty business, but somehow Jolly managed to bring the levity to any interaction. He was good natured, and people feared him simply because so many other people liked him.

With people like Jolly and Deezo on the team, my time as one-double was great. At one point, business was so good, I was thinking buying another vehicle and then renting it out to a driver that couldn't afford a truck. I already knew there is more money to be made with a large unit, so drivers wouldn't mind renting a SUV. I was seeing the other side of the game and began to imagine how much money there was to be made if a person was willing to pay $300 a week just for the privilege of driving a "big boy truck". Yet, as the fall neared, my daughter was coming to live with me. Obviously, I couldn't continue to be out at night working, and leave a 3-year-old home alone. So, when I prayed, I thanked God for blessing me and keeping me safe over the summer, and I asked for a job because Qianna was coming to stay with me. In less than a week, my prayers were answered, and I landed a job with another construction company. On top of that I got a 12 thousand dollar a year bump over my last construction gig. No one can ever tell me that prayers don't work.

After getting hired and working for some time, I swung back through the social club to check on Jolly and let him know that I hadn't forgotten about him. I parked the truck in front of the spot and strolled inside, only to be approached, by a light-skinned dude in his mid-twenties. "What's good Bro? Where is Jolly?" I asked. His expression unmoved, without breaking eye contact and tight lipped he replied, "Who are you?" "It's me. Remember? I was his driver...his OJ." The man's eyes softened while his facial expression remained fixed; it was as if he almost recognized me but wasn't willing to break character. I could tell he was sad but wasn't prepared for what he said next. His eyes now fixed with aggression and squinting almost, he mumbled, "They killed him last week."

Words escaped me as the news of the tragedy echoed in my brain. It is always a travesty when a life is unexpectedly lost or taken; especially when you have known a person and felt their spirit in addition to their physical presence, it can be particularly jarring. This would be my first time dealing with death as an OJ, but certainly not the last. After that, I didn't reach out to any of my other former passengers. None of them had made the connection with me that Jolly had. As tragic as the situation was, I was still alive with responsibilities and the job I was able to land was at a construction management company located about eight blocks from the World Trade Center. What I didn't realize was how my life was going to repeat common themes, in a very a short period of time.

Chapter 2:
99 is Born

On September 11, 2001, the United States suffered the worst act of terrorism, to date, on its soil. The World Trade Center in lower Manhattan was demolished when two commercial airlines were flown directly into the upper levels of both buildings, subsequently killing thousands. Located about eight blocks away, my building literally shook, for a few moments. The lights flickered off and on, when the First tower came crashing to the ground in a plume of debris. Reports would tell of human remains being found in adjacent buildings. Folks were literally "blown" to pieces. That was some terrifying shit. The construction management company that I worked for, had several accounts in the Twin Towers, as well as buildings in the surrounding area. Businesses like Deutsche Bank, and Bank of New York, were large accounts for my company, making up a large chunk of our revenue. After the fact I found out that I was scheduled to manage a renovation project in the Towers in the coming months. It would have been a pretty big deal because, I had never been given the lead, on such a large account. All of that came to a crashing halt. In the aftermath of the attacks, we lost almost sixty percent of our business. I'll never forget trekking through ashes, rubble, and perhaps disintegrated body parts, leaving work for the day, just before noon, on September 11, 2001.

A few months after the attacks, I was transferred to another job site in Red Hook Brooklyn. Due to a lack of work, I eventually found myself laid-off again. At the time, my gross annual salary was $52,000 a year. As I watched the construction industry and the entire country grapple with the economic impact of the terrorist attacks, I knew the chances of me landing another job paying anything close to that, were slim to none.

By this time, two more members had been added to my family. With the addition of my fiancée and her daughter, it grew from Qianna and myself to a full house. Both children, ages six and three, were enrolled in private school which cost $800 per month and with an $1100 per month apartment, etc. etc.... A pay cut was the last thing I could afford. The benefit to my lay-off, and I use that term loosely, was that I was entitled to receive unemployment insurance from the government. Unemployment benefits are normally about two-thirds of your weekly salary, so I figured that all I needed was to find a way to make up the difference. The catch was if I got a job of any sorts that documented tax information, it would cancel my unemployment benefits because obviously, I would no longer be unemployed.

At thirty-one years old, I had no intention of losing everything, I had worked so hard to build. In my mind, taking a pay cut and falling back down the economic ladder was completely unacceptable. Companies, America included, will always give you what you a willing to accept. My belief is once a person accepts less or settles; they get used to settling. Looking back at my life makes me realize that our experiences shape and prepare us for future endeavors. Driving as an OJ for that summer in '99, taught me a hustle that would now allow me to maintain my current standard of living. It also enabled me to keep my sanity for the moment because not being able to handle your responsibilities is stressful. My subconscious told me the construction industry would pick back up and things would return to normal in about a year, so I planned to do the OJ thing until then and then walk away. There is an old saying, "Man plans, and God laughs."

Prior to the terrorist attacks, I was on my way to an early death. The extra income led to a lot of partying, excessive eating, and drinking. Losing my career and potentially my home was the reality check I needed, to shake me out of my stupor . This stint as an OJ lasted for 9 years, and in full disclosure, I can't truthfully speak of it in the past tense because I still have a few loyal passengers that use my services from time to time.

I went to the Chevy dealer and leased Candy brand new. She had 11 miles on the odometer when I went on my test drive. As we speak her dial reads an even 414,414. Candy and I started our second tour of duty July 5, 2002. I went back to my old cab base sadly to discover there was a new one-double, so I settled on 99. With usual Rah flair, it wasn't pronounced ninety-nine, instead it was nine-nine. I was older and had done this type of work before, theoretically things should've been easier for me. Choosing a number one lower my previous was my way of taking a mental step back. Professional athletes say the game slows down for them as they get older. Starting something new or at a more advanced level causes the mind to race as we try to learn the new task. After time spent doing the activity, we adapt, making it easier for you to do. Cause of my prior experience as an OJ, I figured things should be slowed down for me this time around.

I paid the base fees knowing I would be working for a cab base, but not before I worked for myself. My personal rule was, if I was sitting around and somebody called me saying they wanted to put money in my pocket, I was going. One of the perks of working for yourself is being able to decide when to work, and with this being my new way of feeding my family, I figured more often than not, if I answered my phone, I would be going out to get the person that called.

The next day I pulled out of the driveway next to my apartment on Morris Avenue in The Bronx and made a right headed up the block towards 197th Street. I turned on my radio to listen to the dispatcher and hoped to have beginners' luck and catch a call right away. That would be a great way to be welcomed back to the streets. One of the reasons I drive with one hand is because I was always clutching the microphone in my other, waiting to key up. Half of my attention went towards the other drivers and pedestrians, while the other half was listening to B-1 ready to pounce on a call in my area. The block looks like a dead-end, but it turns left so I was deposited on Jerome Avenue and 197th Street. I cruised down Jerome, with Lehman College on my right, headed downtown. Pulling up to the corner of 195th and Jerome, the traffic light turned red bringing me to a halt. I glanced to the left and noticed a pizza shop connected to a laundromat. I thought it was a brilliant idea. Why not have a slice while you wait for your clothes to finish washing?

As the light changed, I made my way to the next corner, Kingsbridge Avenue. The Kingsbridge Armory was on my right. The Armory was built in 1917 to house New York's National Guard's Coast Defense and then the 258th Field Artillery Regiment. Ultimately it was munitions storage, then nothing. In 2013, they announced they had plans to turn it into the world's largest indoor ice center. Kingsbridge Road connects to major arteries. For example, a left on Kingsbridge and you can be on Fordham Road in two minutes. Fordham Road in The Bronx is the home of Fordham University and also a major shopping area, which means people with bags. One thing is for sure, two for certain; people with bags typically need rides home.

A right on Kingsbridge takes me to the Major Deegan Highway in about four minutes. It is the gateway to the world. I didn't have a destination or a call, which compelled me to drive just fast enough to not slow up traffic, but slow enough to not catch lights. Eventually, I figured my best bet would be to park somewhere that I thought should be busy. The spot I chose to start my tour of duty turned out to be Tremont Avenue. Tremont, like Fordham, is a shopping area, but it stretches much further, and covers about seven miles of urban city landscape.

I parked up near Southern Blvd. and Tremont facing east. I figured it was the perfect spot and the proximity to Southern Blvd. allowed access to the South Bronx. I could be there in a matter of five minutes on "first shout," then definitely ten minutes on "second shout." The time was about 1 PM. In retrospect, I should have known that was way too early in the day for me to be in the streets trying to get money the day after Independence Day. After all, it was a national holiday, and I was positive everyone went out the night before. Realistically, the next day kept most people in their homes eating left-over barbecue, especially after hanging out all night. I guess the excitement of making runs made me jump the gun. The airwaves were quiet. During radio silence, some of the drivers wait at a place known as "The Pound." It's nothing glorious, it's just a parking lot where drivers hang out. Our Pound was in the parking area that used to be shared by Burger King and Pathmark supermarket just off of the Bruckner Expressway. Pathmark, which used to be a staple in a few neighborhoods across the country, started going out of business. They definitely were not going to make it through the year. I sometimes passed through The Pound, but seldom spent time there. I wasn't in the streets to be socializing, but maybe kicking it with them cats would've made things easier for me. They could have definitely given me a few pointers. At the end of the day, I was in these streets to make money, and if I was talking and standing in a parking lot, I wasn't driving and definitely wasn't making no fuckin money.

Being part of a base is not just about waiting for calls. The base should become like an extended family to you. If one of our fellow drivers were to ever throw out a distress call, we would all rush to their aid. Thankfully I have never had a make that shout to the dispatcher, but if I had, the block would have been swarmed with all different types of units in a matter of minutes. One of my passengers, Dap from Clay Avenue, told me a tale about when there was once a problem with a driver on their block. A near riot wound up breaking out when his friends from the base arrived . Dap would go on to tell me that my base's owner, Duke, was on the block fighting that day alongside the other drivers. I never asked Duke about that, but why would a regular dude from the street be telling me tales.

The fact that he knew my base's owner by name gave his story credence.

When I did occasionally chill at The Pound, I was a sponge, soaking up all the information I could for those short visits. The other drivers were the network before networking was a thing. Almost everything was accessible, especially car stereos or any other auto accessories. They were the best resources even if all I wanted to ask was which neighborhoods were cool to roll through. Base time was only mandatory for driver meetings, and the penalty for missed meetings was a fine. Meetings came with at least a couple days' notice, so it was hard to miss one if you didn't have car trouble, or something else going on outside of the city. Even then, those were excusable. Any missed fine meant drivers were on "No Copy" status until they paid their fines. One time we had a quick, fifteen-minute meeting in the parking lot of the Whitestone Movie Theater that used to be on the Bruckner Expressway. Picture one minute there is regular traffic flowing into a parking lot, then suddenly about forty vehicles of all different makes and models roll up and converge within a five-minute period. I am surprised that the police never rolled up on us to see what all of us were doing huddled together like that.

Outside of the meetings, most of the drivers rarely met each other. There are some instances when a customer would call the base requesting more than one unit because their group is too large to fit into just one. When that happens, most drivers will chat briefly since they will be driving in tandem. The only other time that I can think of running into another driver would be when we came to pay base fee.

During radio silence, I would occasionally key up to make sure that I was still connected to the base. Back in '99 when I was an OJ, I remember very little radio silence. In those days the B-1 was constantly throwing out calls. I know we're a long way from that, but regardless it was surprising not to hear anything at all coming from the base.

After about a half hour of silence, the B-1 comes over the air waves and throws out a local call, meaning they were within the vicinity of the base. I was only about five minutes from the area, and I wasn't comfortable going over there to pick up people. Safety wasn't a concern as much as my ability to navigate that side of The Bronx. All the streets had names, which was very confusing. As opposed to the westside of The Bronx or say Manhattan, which have numbers on the street to let you know if you were going uptown or downtown. There weren't any numbers, and I wasn't used to the avenues only having names. Don't get me wrong, I could break out my map and find the location. However, when trying to beat other drivers to the punch, a brother doesn't have time to be looking up addresses. To give an estimated time of arrival, you must know where you are going or at least what direction you are going in.

A lot of our business came from the zone, the ten-block radius around base, so the majority of the drivers hung out around there. While that logic was completely understandable, I chose the other side of town because fewer drivers meant less competition. For what it is worth, I love the road less travelled. Being parked on Tremont seemed like as good a place as any. I didn't want to go too far down into the South Bronx because I wouldn't be able to reach calls in the upper Bronx. Passengers calling from areas like Gun Hill Road & 230th Street would be out of range for me. During the three hours at that spot on Tremont, I didn't come close to catching a call.

The B-1 spoke fast, but after a while it slows down in your mind, and you can hear them as clear as day. Even though I had been an OJ three years prior, it was like learning a new language all over again. The only difference was this time I had no Los to hold my hand and key up to get me calls until I got the swing of things. This time it was just me parked on Tremont in a shiny new truck with less than seventy miles on the odometer. As the day rolled on the pressure began to mount. Three became four hours, and I hadn't made a dime. I was so desperate, the thought of picking up a stranger standing curbside hailing a cab crossed my mind more than a few times. I had a family at home depending on me, and as things stood, my fiancée already thought I was crazy for doing this; as opposed to the same boring routine of applying for work and getting a "real job." After being laid off, I told a couple of the folks at my old job about my new career as a driver. Multiple people responded, "No seriously, what are you going to do about a job?" I refused to let their doubts become mine. I stood firm on that as another hour passed, and at about 6 PM, I heard the perfect call. I was only about five blocks away from where the woman wanted to be picked up, so I pounced on "first shout." She was a Spanish woman in her mid to late 40's.

My go to conversation starter with a passenger was a standard greeting followed by asking how they felt. Most people responded, while some are indifferent to exchanging pleasantries and don't say anything. She responded, and I had been sitting in the truck alone for five hours, so it felt great to actually talk to another person. "How you doing?" she asked in a thick Puerto Rican accent. Her voice was sweet and harmonic, like a jazz singer's. It had the tone of someone who had lived and knew things. She was definitely somebody's mom because she had a motherly nature about her. Not to mention the Fupa. She was genuinely interested, and not just exchanging pleasantries. "I'm fine," I responded. "It's my first day, and I've been in the car for about five hours with no calls, but I'm cool. You're my first passenger, shoutout to you." She chuckled and wiggled back and forth in her seat like she was dancing, and with a smile replied, "Well, I call the base all the time. It's okay, it's like that sometimes but just hang in there and you will be fine." She smiled, paid me, and got out of Candy. I got a measly eight dollars for that trip, and regardless of if she called the base our paths never crossed again. Considering the amount of tender, that eight bucks was nothing to the priceless words of encouragement she gave me.

I didn't return to Tremont after dropping her off, it made no sense to waste the gas to get back to a particular spot. I parked on College Avenue to wait for my next call. There was no particular reason or logical rationale that I picked College Avenue; I was close. A lot of thought went into picking my spot to begin my shift and it netted me a whopping eight dollars. Why not just pick a random location and stop to see what the streets have in store for me? Well, the streets are cold every time, and I will tell you what the streets had in store for me…Nothing.

I stayed out until about 10 PM and went back home with eight dollars made. It was not the debut I had in mind at all. On my way home, I was trying to prepare a way to tell my lady, I stayed out ten hours and made eight dollars. It would be an understatement to say I didn't second, third, and fourth guess my decision to not reenter the standard workforce. Every time I would come back to the same conclusion. As I spoke to reassure my soon to be wife, I was also convincing myself that everything would be ok.

As I laid down to sleep at the end of that first night, I was thankful for making it home safely. I spoke to God and asked that He continue to watch over me and help me get this paper going forward. It's not a good idea to pray to God for money. He may give you what you ask for at a high cost. After making eight dollars in a day, I was willing to do almost anything to get paid. I had no idea exactly how soon after God was going to call my bluff.

Chapter 3:
2000 Valentine Ave.

Day two was a Friday. One of my first thoughts when I woke up for my second day back "on the grind" was how not to repeat the shitty outcome of the day before. I understand that life has ups and downs and somedays are rainy, even if it's sunny. Day number one was the rain, day number two was the bounce back. I was hitting the streets looking for a little bit of sunshine.

My daily goal when I left the house was $100 profit. That was the minimum amount that I could come home with and feel like I had a decent day at the office. That's not to say, that once my quota is reached, I was going home. On the contrary, I was known to stay out in the streets and surpass it. The more the merrier, especially in matters concerning money. The quota was developed as a cutoff point. Working for yourself meant that you're making your own hours, and it was very easy to go overboard. If you wanted to be a workaholic, and basically live in your vehicle, you could do that. If you only wanted to work a few hours a day, you could do that too.

With a family at home, I couldn't be in the street working all the time. I had to spend quality time with them, and I needed some "me" time. During my personal time I didn't want to be concerned with going to pick anyone up or do anything for anyone else but me. Learning how to juggle my family, my business and myself would prove to be really challenging.

Before I left the house on day two, I laid down a schedule I thought would work for me and my family. The family needed to know when daddy would be around and when he wouldn't. I learned the error of my ways after looking back on day one and realized that heading out into the streets that early definitely wasn't a good idea. Unless it is the weekend, chances are the afternoons would be pretty dead. People who have regular jobs are at work during those hours, and folks that are out in the street all hours of the night are sleeping.

It was about 4 PM when I kissed my fiancée and kids goodbye and headed out. I was intentional about doing things differently. I pulled out of the driveway and had no choice but to make the same right as the day before and follow Morris Avenue half a block north as it wraps around to Jerome and 197th street. Jerome Avenue, presented options. A left turn went past the Armory, likely to conjure up memories of a disappointing day one. One block north of the right turn on Jerome Avenue at 198th meant, with another right, I was two blocks from the Grand Concourse.

The Grand Concourse is just as its name implies. It is one of the main arteries of The Bronx. The Concourse begins at the Northside of The Bronx near Tracy Towers. Tracy Towers is a group of about six or seven apartment buildings and are located just off the Hudson River. Each building stretches approximately forty stories into the sky, giving some lucky tenants a great view. It was considered state of the art when it first opened in the mid-1970s. While the view is still the same, the quality of life has slipped just as it has in many places across the country. The Grand Concourse slices through the heart of the West Bronx, coming to a finish at the Madison Avenue Bridge on 138th Street. A quick skip across the bridge would lead me into the heart of Harlem if needed. Along the way, I could easily make a left or a right, and connect to any of the popular veins flowing east or west through The Bronx. The option to go not only north and south, but east and west as well at the blink of an eye was a bonus in picking this spot to chill.

When I put the car in park, I told myself if the B-1 threw out a call, I was going to key up for it if I could understand what they were saying. Since I was a new driver, the base allowed me a grace period to find the addresses. I was trying, and it was safe to say for the first couple of weeks, when "nine-nine" ran a time of five minutes, it would be more like ten to fifteen. Some drivers are notoriously late. For a beginner, being late is understandable. Sometimes drivers key up for a call knowing they can't be there on time. Even though the base gave me some leeway as a newbie, I never took advantage. I know that I wouldn't appreciate my driver being late. While cruising the Concourse, I heard a call at an address about eight minutes away, so I didn't key up on the five minute "first shout." The minute the B-1 started her voice for the "second shout," I went berserk keying up with my trigger finger. Normally keying up over the B-1 would lead to a verbal lashing and denial of the call. However, on nine-nine's second day, it was all good. "Nine-Nine ten minutes, Nine-Nine?" Stammering a bit, "Posi..uhh..positive," came out of my mouth. The call was a pickup for a woman and her two children heading to a different section of the borough. The cost of the ride was $15, and in under a half an hour my party had been picked up and dropped off. The woman got out of Candy with a smile while handing me a twenty-dollar bill to keep. It was a nice little tip to start the day. It was about 5 PM, I had been in the streets for one hour and made $20. It was a beautiful summer afternoon with not a cloud in the sky. Indeed, the sun appeared to be coming out.

Shortly after the first fare was dropped off, B-1 threw out a call that was exactly two blocks away. The pickup was on Vyse Avenue and 178th Street. There was a stark contrast between day one and day two. As I keyed up for the second call, a wave of relief washed over my body. Sounding like a seasoned vet, I answered, "Nine-Nine, one minute." The bad part about taking a call on "first shout" is that you don't get to hear who you are picking up or where they are going. In the pursuit, of dollars and cents, it didn't really matter. The passengers were two Black men, about twenty years old; one sat in the front as the other dude quietly slid into the backseat.

The guy in the front was excitable and animated much like a child on Christmas. He did the majority of the talking as he chattered on aimlessly about the weather and quickly veering the conversation towards the attractive women he spotted walking up along the sidewalk. He seemed easily distracted. He rambled, "You know, me and my Bro," he pointed to the quiet dude in the back seat, "We're going to the club later, I could call you back if you want to give me your number. We're gonna need a ride." "Bet. I got you," I replied as cool as I possibly could to hold the excitement. I was open to any avenues of money I could find, and it felt like I was already on the road. Whether he called the base or not, direct access to me could mean more bank. This was exactly what the job was supposed to be. It was a beautiful day, the music in Candy was on point per usual, and the fare was cool and potentially paying me again, later. We chatted back and forth as we rode to our destination, 2000 Valentine Avenue.

As soon as we pulled up to the location, they guy in the front quickly unbuckled his seatbelt, looked at me square in my eyes and said, "I will be right back," as he hopped out grinning. Throughout all the conversation I shared with his brother on the trip over, homie in the backseat stayed quiet. That's understandable, there are plenty of families with a chatty sibling, and a more laid back one. When his bother exited Candy, he remained quietly seated in his rear passenger side seat. I quickly glanced in my rearview mirror in hopes of making eye contact, to start a conversation. I wasn't worried, but the quiet was a bit unusual at this point because he was sitting there as quietly as he had been since they climbed in the car. I sat there for about thirty-seconds, scanning my other mirrors and watching traffic when I looked in my rearview, and then back to the sideview mirror on my drivers' side, and I saw a short Latino guy in full sprint towards my truck wielding a samurai sword over his head. I quickly slammed Candy into drive and screeched off into up the block. I didn't care why he was running towards me; I didn't even know him. What I did know is that I needed to get the fuck out of there as soon as possible.

As we drove north on Valentine Avenue, I passed three police cars speeding down the block towards me with lights flashing and sirens blaring. Hopefully they were going to bag that asshole running around The Bronx with a katana. We had driven roughly half a block when I looked in my rearview mirror, this time noticing police cars racing up behind me. They seemingly appeared out of thin air. I knew I didn't do anything wrong. Maybe they wanted to talk to me about the Latino Ninja, so I stopped to try and figure out what was going on.

Before I could put Candy in park, an officer popped up in my peripheral off to my left about seven to ten feet away. Gun drawn, he yelled at me, "Let me see your fucking hands." I'm no firearms expert, but I feel like I would know good form if I saw it. There he was standing with his feet firmly planted, about shoulders width apart in perfect form; there was no doubt in my mind that he would pull the trigger.

I stuck both of my hands out of the window with my foot on the break and yelled, "The car is still in drive! I don't want to reach!" Another officer ran up to my truck door, put Candy in park and snatched me out of the driver's seat. The officer began patting me down and asking the usual questions in a search for weapons or drugs. After finding nothing, he led me to the back of Candy, near the hatch, and placed me down on the concrete on my knees. The officers huddled with each other for several minutes, talking without making any noticeable gestures or movements. After they recognized I wasn't a risk or a threat, they allowed me to stand. A tall white undercover officer walked over to me and began to fill me in on the situation. "While you were driving up the avenue, the guy in the backseat threw a gun out of the window," he said in serious tone, understanding I had no idea. I couldn't believe it.

Those two guys had been riding around robbing people. They would call the base so they could show up in a different unit each time they went out. Imagine two random people climbing out of a mysterious vehicle and trying to rob you as you walked down the block. I'm not sure what is more shocking for the victims, the fact that two people randomly hopped out of a car to rob them, or the fact they're being robbed. The worst part is that after they stick you up at gunpoint, they drive off; and it's next to impossible to give a description of the vehicle to the cops because there aren't any identifying logos. Perhaps they lived in the area and kept returning after each heist. In retrospect, I always wondered how the police and the Latino Ninja knew that those two guys would be pulling up. They were obviously waiting for us. I often thought maybe the guy in the front was trying to get away from the quiet guy in the back. Perhaps he was being "forced" to go along with the robbing spree. Who knows ?

As they led the guy away in handcuffs, the escorting detective turned and looked at me square in the eyes, asking "Do you know who you had in your car?" Incredulously he continued, "You are fucking stupid." That was the last thing he said before walking away. The words bounced right off me because I knew I wasn't stupid. A man on a mission to provide for his family is not stupid, regardless of what choices he may make. The encounter was jarring and humbling all at once. I was grateful to have gotten out of that alive, but it was a sobering reality check as opposed to the high I felt when they got in the car. Now, I was standing alone in the middle of the street on a hot summer night with a block full of people staring at me. I gathered the few CD's which had been thrown on the ground as the officers rummaged around looking for a weapon and got back in the truck. While starting Candy, I noticed she had little less than one hundred miles on the odometer.

Interactions with police for Black people are all too often hit or miss. I consider myself blessed and highly favored to have driven away from the scene that day. After absolutely nothing happening on the first day, the second day had enough action to last me the next five years. I wasn't about to go home and cry in a pillow though. God was testing me to see if I had faith or if I would tuck my tail between my legs and run away. At this point I was all in .

The time was about 8 PM and replaying the events of the day were starting to wear on me. Traumatizing events sometimes trigger emotional or physiological responses from your past. Effectively, trauma stops your brain at the time of the event, but I wasn't going to let this stop me. However, it did send me down the rabbit hole. While I was still an undergrad in Washington DC, I had a police officer push me to the ground and stick his gun to the base of my head, right behind my right ear. The day I felt that cold steel up against my flesh was the day I came to terms with my own mortality. As disheartening as it was, what I had just gone through somehow desensitized me to violence and death. I often say , " once you come face to face, with the Grim Reaper, living is a piece of cake."

"Base time is 8:05 PM. I need a 165 and Clay." The B-1's voice darted over the radio, snapping me back to reality. I wasn't as fast with the trigger finger this time. I learned my lesson the hard way and figured it wiser to hear who and what I was possibly getting myself into. On "second shout," I heard there were two males on Clay Avenue going on a slight hold. One would think, after what I had just gone through, I might be a bit leery about picking up males. Well, I wasn't. I knew my intentions were pure and I felt like I had nothing to fear. I keyed up and was made positive for the two males on Clay.

Pulling up at the address on Clay Avenue between 164th and 165th Streets, I found a stocky wheat-complexioned man who looked like he was in his late twenties standing in front of the building. He paused for a moment to make sure I was his ride before he stepped up to the truck. As he climbed in the front, a teenager that looked closer to fourteen than eighteen followed suit into the back. The guy in the front seat went by the name of Dap, and the youngster in the called himself Al. Al could've been short for a plethora of names, and honestly there is no telling if his real name even started with an A. Dap was speaking for both of them and told me they had about three or four stops to make. Dap and I talked as he made his stops across The Bronx. At each stop, Dap would hop out of Candy and run over to talk to someone for a few minutes, and then come back and get in the car. When I brought them back to Clay Avenue, Dap smiled and asked, "What you got goin on later? You gonna be busy?" "I'll be busy working, what's good?" The words flew out of my mouth without a second thought. I knew I had a wild day, but hopefully , Dap and Al didn't plan on throwing any guns out of the window.

"I gotta make a run up to Kingston. How much you would charge me?" he cheerfully asked. I had no idea where Kingston was so I couldn't begin to give him a price. "Where's Kingston?" I asked. "Right near…well not too far from Woodbury Commons," he replied. From what I knew, Woodbury Commons was about an hour and a half away. He owed me $25 from the time we were together already. I rubbed my chin as if I was pondering deep in thought, with a final scratch of my chin hair, I turned to him and said, "I got you for one-fifty. That's including the twenty-five you owe me from us being out just now." "Oh, I love that price," Dap laughed. "Nine-nine, you, my nigga. That's a good number too. I'm gonna hit you in a minute." True to his word, a couple of hours later, we were off on our way to Kingston. Life is funny like that. One minute you're down, then suddenly the right opportunity knocks, and just that fast, you're back on the upswing.

It was a smooth ride up to Kingston. At the time, my mom was still in Spring Valley, north across the Tappan Zee bridge. When I saw Woodbury Commons, I knew that we were close and a little ways more and we were at the exit for Kingston, NY.

The house we landed at is where Dap's little brother was staying with a younger lady he had hooked up with. Besides wanting to see his younger sibling, Dap took some weed for them to smoke and sell. When out of town, meaning away from the big city, good weed is always in short supply. At the same time, he didn't take a large amount of weed up there with him on that trip. It was enough to net them about $1,000 after it was all said and done. Don't get me wrong, in the hood, that thousand can really stretch to seem like more than it is; so, for some it's worth the small risk when considering the penalties and jail time for sale and possession. After dropping Dap in Kingston, I drove back down the highway headed to my apartment in The Bronx. It was about 5 AM when I walk thru the door. I was tired, but I still felt great. Entering the bedroom, my fiancée casually turned over in the bed. I tried to be quiet out of fear of waking her up. She stirred gently, nestling against the soft white pillowcase. She was awake already. I don't know if I woke her up or if she stayed up all night worrying about me, either way I felt her relief as she opened her eyes and smiled at me. "So how did you do baby?" I reached into my pocket and peeled off five twenty-dollar bills. "Here's my contribution," I replied with a smile. "Oh my…How'd you get all that?" she groggily asked with a smile. "Grinding," was my single word response. "I'm out here," I added with a grin. I definitely had no intention on telling her what I went through. There would be no mention of the stick-up kids, or Latino Ninja, or good shooting-formed cop that was ready to murder me. My experiences from that day, with those guys and with those cops earlier was a secret, securely tucked away in my memory banks, until now.

I laid down to sleep after that second night for the first time on what would be my third day. In disbelief, under my breath I muttered to myself, "You had a crazy fuckin day Bro. Good shit." In two days, I had run the gauntlet of emotions and experienced what I perceived as the worse things that could happen to a driver. I spent a whole day in the streets only to make eight dollars, only to follow that up with nothing short of a day that I couldn't make up if I tried. Life imitates art and art imitates life in a cyclical pattern. I remember going to sleep thinking, "I definitely need to write about this one day."

Chapter 4:
BLOODs and Sco

That first summer taught me more than I wanted to learn about the streets. Looking back, I am thankful for the experiences and the access gained to a world that most people will never know. We hear stories from all over the world about underworlds of other countries. However, this story has the uniqueness of a story only possible in America. New York City had morphed into a perfect storm of chaos. Unemployment was high and large numbers of people were on the brink of desperation and fringes of society, scrapping to get by. New York has the third highest cost of living in the United States, so it's no wonder why NYC is dubbed the "the city that never sleeps." Everyone is trying to earn a buck to survive.

I laid in bed, thinking about how my first two days on the job got rid of any fears that I could have had hidden inside, and I knew things could only get better. The universe is full of endless possibilities and, day two was full of things I never would have considered before. I put my best foot forward knowing the worst was behind me and began living with more gratitude than ever. If madness like that was capable of happening at any given moment, I figured that I might as well go hard. Worst case scenario was I died, and if it happened, at least I was doing my best attempt at providing for my family. If you do your best, you'll be rewarded. It may not be what you want, but it will be what you deserve.

I needed to get in Candy and get back in the streets. Nothing was going to make the memories of the first two days disappear faster than getting back out there and making new ones. After a couple of weeks, I fell into a bit of a pattern.

My work schedule was now set in stone. I worked from Wednesday through Saturday and rested on Sundays. Mondays and Tuesdays are usually pretty quiet on the base. During summers, kids are on break and sometimes parents would take their kids to the pool or something fun on one of those days; but for the most part, it was a lot of waiting. Air conditioners in any car requires the vehicle to be on, and that means sitting idle and burning gas. Gas is a necessary expense in this business and is not to be wasted. Truthfully, the work week started on Wednesdays only because the base fee is due on Thursday. I could have easily gone into my own pocket for the $70 for the base fee, but my rule was to make the streets pay for themselves. Once money was in the house it was put aside for the family. Any pocket money I might've needed, whether it was for gas, or in this instance the base fee, came strictly out of my immediate earnings. Typically, I would leave the house with $10 in my pocket; one five-dollar bill and five singles, and that was just enough to make change for a passenger.

When Dap from Clay Avenue got back in town, he made it a point to call me and say, "Nine – Nine – this is D.A." "It's who?" I asked. "It's me. D.A., the dude you took upstate a few weeks ago." I didn't recognize the voice until he told me about the trip upstate, then I knew who he was. Some brothers on the street go by multiple names. "You busy?" Dap asked. "If you're not, I want you to come check me." I was sitting in Candy waiting on a call as I still spent most of my time doing, so I was more than happy to go check Dap and make some quick cash. "Nah I'm chillin. I don't have a call or nothing. I'll be there in a second," I responded. I put Candy in drive and pulled off. When I pulled up on the block of 165th and Clay Avenue, it felt weird. It's amazing how different a landscape can look with the change of night and day. Everything looked and felt different as if I had never been there before, and there was no physical difference outside of the time of day. This trip was in the late afternoon as opposed to midnight, and 165th Street and Clay had a vibrance that I had never experienced. The corner store was open and bustling with activity, and it looked no different from a typical summer scene in New York City, with people of all ages out and about, and milling around.

I pulled up to the curb and parked several yards past the corner store when Dap suddenly popped out of the building. He was with by two young males that appeared to be in their late teens, and at max, early twenties. Climbing into the front, Dap immediately extended, his right hand to me. We slapped hands and locked fingers in traditional dap form as I asked, "What's good Bro?" "We gotta run the little homie over to see his girl real quick," he said as he gestured to one of the boys in the backseat. I recognized him. The little homie he motioned to had been introduced as Al the last time I was with them, but Dap never introduced the other kid to me. Usually, if someone doesn't get an introduction in the streets, the person in irrelevant. It's rude, but so are the streets. People had been using the term "homie" for as long as I could remember, but there's always layers to etymology. I later found out that when some people use the word, they're referring to a fellow gang member of the BLOODs.

Originally the BLOODS were founded in LA in the late 1960's. Growing up in New York City during the 70's and

80's, the Spanish community had gangs such as the Latin Kings, but in Black neighborhoods, there was no real unified gang presence to speak of. Dap and his little homies needed a quick ride over to Westchester Avenue; it's a few blocks from the number six subway line. Al was dropping off some money to his girlfriend to go clothes shopping. "I gotta keep my shawty looking fresh," he said proudly as we were in route. The funny thing is, I had to park up the block because her mother didn't want her hanging around "that type." Go figure.

In the early 90's, inside the prison system of New York City, the East coast BLOODs were founded. The Black inmates needed a way to protect themselves against abuses done to them by the much more numerous and organized Spanish gangs. They organized themselves inside the prison walls, with the intention of controlling things both inside and out under the name United Blood Nation. As the members were released, the gang took on a life of its own. The first set popped up in The Bronx on 183rd Street and before you knew it there were different sets popping up all over the city. Eventually their tentacles would stretch up and down the East coast. Rumor had it that at the time the original BLOODs out in California didn't acknowledge these loosely knit organizations on the East coast as being real BLOODs. One of the sets called the area surrounding Clay Avenue home. One block to the east of Clay Avenue, on Webster Avenue beginning at 165th Street, lie a cluster of public housing projects which at the time was a pulse of BLOOD gang activity.

I was getting back in the streets after years of a being "a square", barely breaking any laws. I had no idea that any of this gang stuff was going on around me. Since I hung out in neighborhoods all over the city all throughout my teens and twenties, I always considered myself to be street smart ,; but BLOODs on the East coast caught me completely off guard. If I didn't know what was going on, imagine how lost a true square would be.

If people believed everything the media showed, the assumption would be it's very easy to spot a BLOOD by the bright red ensemble they were wearing with the red bandana on their head. Thankfully we don't because the reality was nothing like that. On the East coast, they figured out broadcasting your gang affiliation to anyone paying attention wasn't a good idea. Gang colors in high gang activity areas made them easily identifiable for your rival and police. If there is any violent crime in the area, who do you think the first person to be picked up and questioned will be? So, in the hood, the identifying markers were known only to members of the gang. For example, the original game cap of the Washington Nationals was a gang marker. It's a red cap with the white "W" on it. The alternate Boston Red Sox was one as well.

During my years in the streets, I have come across all types of BLOODs. Maybe I should say people claiming to be a BLOOD. Gang culture is interesting because in some areas it's completely segregated, and the gangs are formed based on the ethnic group. In places like New York City, it is based on your hood, and is a blend of the ethnic groups in the area. I have met Black dudes like my boys Ren and Butch that claim to be BLOOD and Spanish guys like the ones from 145th Street between Brook and St. Ann's Avenues that called themselves BLOOD. I even met a white kid named "Red" from midtown Manhattan that was a 16-year-old BLOOD, at the time. I was puzzled. Who would have thought there would be a skinny white boy from midtown, calling himself BLOOD?

I met a young homie named Justice who was seventeen when we met, from 143rd Street between Willis and 3rd Avenues. "Just" was his moniker on the streets, and he weighed a wiry 150 pounds and stood about five foot eight. However, out of all the measurables in the world, there was no way to measure the amount of heart beating inside of this kid's chest. Despite his small stature, that kid could throw hands with the best of them. There's a story about the day a beat-cop tried to put his hands on him during another typical day of harassment. It took three officers to get him to the ground, and at the end of it all Just didn't have anything on him just as he had told the officer when altercation initially began. "Stop and frisk" as they call it, was just another way to escalate the tension in the hood between cops and citizens. It basically gives cops the option to detain us for whatever they deem "suspicious." When they decide to detain, question, and harass folks, they will. It doesn't matter if they have probable cause or not, and hopefully you get to walk away and tell the story instead of being driven away to the coroner.

I respected the lil homie for his fighting skills, and when it came time for him to get that money, that boy would grind for three or four days straight. If there were fiends in the street with money to spend, Just was out there. He would always say, "Other people go home after they get a certain amount of

money. I'm staying out until there is no more money to get."
I love that work ethic and at times, I feel the same way about
driving.

The whole round trip took maybe forty minutes. After
the ride was over, Dap got out and walked around the front of
Candy, to approach the driver's window and said, "Son, dead
ass, it would be a good idea to stay close to the area because
there is always someone trying to go somewhere on my block.
If you make yourself a regular face in the hood muthafuckas
are gonna to make sure you eat. Be safe." He dapped me
again and walked away. I had no reason to doubt Dap or any
loyalty to a particular spot, so I started making Clay Avenue a
drive thru block of mine anytime I was in the area.

On one of those occasional times, I was passing through
Clay Avenue, I stopped at the corner store for a few snacks
and some water. As I was walking back to my vehicle, I was
approached by a guy in his early twenties who said, "Yo G,
I seen you in the hood riding with Dap. I gotta make a run
and was wondering if you could take me and the homies on
a slight hold real quick?" "Yeah, I got you Bro," I replied.
"That is why I am here." He waved for his boys to come over,
and they climbed in the truck. I never got names; the one that
approached me said, "You can just drive around the corner and
park across the street." I followed his directions and parked.
I looked up and I noticed that we were sitting across from an
auto repair shop. It was about 5 PM, and after sitting there for
about five minutes, he said, "Drive around the block for me." I
drove around the block again, this time the kid sitting in front
said, "Stop right here next to the parking garage on the right."

I stopped. As we were waiting, a late model BMW pulled out of the lot and turned onto the street. "Follow that car," he said. I assumed it was a friend of theirs, we were following so I did. As we were driving, I noticed the route we were on was taking us towards the highway but paid it no mind, and then we were on to the highway. This was no longer slight hold; we were in traffic and the clock was already ticking past an hour. At this point, I was trying to figure out where we were going, so I said, "Bro we're past the hour, how much are y'all planning on paying me for this little adventure?" The kid in the front seat said, "The guy that we're following is the owner of that repair shop that we were sitting in front of. Now, I had heard that he took the money from the shop home with him at the end of the week. We're going to follow him to his exit in Connecticut and rob him."

Something exploded inside of me, I'm not sure what emotion it was but it was a sudden rush of thoughts. They're either crazy or stupid, or both! Have you ever been to the suburbs? Do you know how quiet the streets are in suburbia? If they think that I am going down in this harebrained scheme, they are out of their fucking minds. In the fifty-seconds it took me to process what he said, I composed a concise thought to respond with. I opened my mouth and said firmly, "I am not cut out for this." "Well, we don't have any money. So, if you want to get paid you better keep up with that vehicle," he replied coldly. I know that I said I was willing to do almost anything to feed my family, almost, being the key word. I wasn't about to be an accessory to armed robbery in Connecticut, so I simply let his car "get away" from me in traffic. It wasn't hard to do since it was rush hour, with traffic all over the place. I rerouted, returned to Clay Avenue and dropped them off where I picked them up. Needless-to-say, I wasn't their favorite driver after that. Later I saw Dap and told him the story to which Dap's response was, "Don't pick up anyone on this block unless I tell you they're ok." I really would've appreciated that little tip in the beginning, when he told me what a great idea it would be for me to hang around.

Later in that summer, while out on a Friday night, I heard a shout come across my radio, "I need a Gun Hill - White Plains. I need a Gun Hill – White Plains, one male. 3rd and last shout I need a Gun Hill – White Plains, one male going to Tremont and Webster Avenues – the Rumba." The Rumba, as I would come to find out was a reggae dance hall. Other drivers were hesitant about picking up the call because its origin was the Gun Hill Projects. True to its name, the Gun Hill Housing Projects were no stranger to "getting it popping" from time to time. I was extremely naïve to The Bronx streets and keyed up for the call. I thought, "It's just one male, how dangerous can he be?" As it turned out my passenger wasn't dangerous at all. The one male ended up being a kid that went by the street name of Sco . Sco, was short for Rosco, like the character from the 80's sitcom, "The Dukes of Hazzard." In the sitcom, Rosco was the Sheriff. Perhaps Sco was trying to typecast himself as the sheriff of the hood, or maybe he was just looking for something that sounded cool and original. Given names are rarely used in the hood.

In time, the eighteen-year-old Sco that I picked up that night would come to be known as "Sco da Criminal." On the night I met Sco, way back in 2002, he was just a kid going to the club to try and rub up on some Jamaican booty. Who could blame him? Sco was a happy-go-lucky kid who wanted to have a good time. After he got into the truck, he told me how he had been calling the base for over half an hour, trying in vain to get someone to come and get him. Sco is the one that explained to me how his projects had a violent reputation, therefore a lot of drivers were hesitant to come there to get people that they didn't know. That call couldn't have been easier for me. The only trouble that Sco was trying to get into was between some chick's legs. He was so happy I came to get him that he gave me $20 for a $12 ride. Sco exited the vehicle and said, "Yo, give me your number, I'm definitely going to call you again. I rap, and I'm always going to shows and shit." I didn't think anything of it because every hood has rappers and basketball players, and most of them aren't ever any good.

Many of our youths have settled upon the idea that the only way they can succeed in life or have access to wealth is through rap music or sports. I have been guilty of thinking that some of them never possessed the concept of simply getting a good education and then blazing a path in society. The reality is access to wealth is limited, and our inner-city youths see those as the easiest access points because they are using their natural gifts. The sadder reality is our school systems aren't designed for their success; and while trades and other skills will always be utilized, they are often viewed as the lesser option. One could blame capitalism, either way, success is relative, and statistics show their chances of "making it" are much higher if they aren't relying on a career as a rapper or an athlete.

Well, as it stands, Sco was one of the best underground rappers in New York City, and I am tempted to say in the country. I remember a time I picked him up after he had just gotten back from a battle in Chicago. I was intrigued. Sco was traveling halfway across the country to battle, and couldn't help myself from blurting out mid story, "Did you win?" He snickered and without hesitation replied, "Come on Rah, you know I don't lose."

Later that summer, Sco called me to his block because he wanted to use Candy as a prop in a music video. The shoot had been organized by his de facto manager Chino, who was in a relationship at the time with Sco's sister, Ronda. They eventually had a son together, and to this day, I still believe Ronda is the best female rapper that I have ever heard. When I arrived on the block to pick Sco up for his shoot, I immediately noticed that he was wearing a navy blue, bandana on his head. I knew right away Sco was repping CRIP gang. CRIPs, like the BLOODs, started on the West Coast but had somehow migrated and sprung up here on the East Coast. I asked Sco, "Are You a CRIP?" "Yes," he replied in his casual fashion. "You are the first CRIP that I have met," I chimed back. "I am in a neighborhood surrounded by BLOODs. I'm different, I'm not a follower. I am me. If all of them wanted to be BLOODs, I said fine I'll be a CRIP," he said assertively. That pretty much summed up everything I needed to know about this kid's character. He was certainly no punk, because it takes a lot of courage to dare to be different in any situation, especially something that's neighborhood gang related. It was practically suicide to go against the tide of a gang which has swept up your whole hood. To this day, I think they probably let him get away with that because of his talent which was known all throughout the area.

I'm not here to judge anyone and the choices that they make with their lives. As long as I'm treated with respect, we will never have a problem. I am glad to say, over a decade later, Sco is still someone I would consider a friend of mine, and I wish him nothing but the best because he is genuinely a good dude .

Sco had been arrested a few times, and actually served time at one point and; all of his offenses were drug related. I feel there is a difference between drug-related offenses and violent felonies. Sco would serve one year here or maybe eighteen months there, and as soon as Sco was released, either to a half-way house or the streets, the first thing that he always did was holler at me. I am not even in the business of driving people around nearly as heavy as I once was, and Sco still calls me to see if I am available from time to time.

When we met, he was just beginning to get his rap career off the ground. I am a child of the rap generation meaning that I saw the birth of Hip-Hop, before the mainstream media coined the term rap. As a fan of the art since its inception, it gives me a unique perspective; and from the first time I heard Sco rap, I knew that he was indeed a rapper, and not just a "wanna be" like many others. Sco was without management, and to me, based on my business background, it seemed as though I would be a logical choice to fill that position. I had no experience as a music manager, but that wasn't a deterrent to me. "You should let me manage you," I said to him candidly.

"I can represent you." "You know what you doing?" He asked. "You're an OJ."

I was a little annoyed that he was underestimating my capabilities or "judging the book by the cover," so to speak, but it didn't matter. I looked at him with a straight face and sternly said, "I have a strong background in business, and I know how to hustle. I know and meet all types of people, and I can do a lot better for you than you can do all by yourself. If I get you a deal, I get a percentage and if I don't you don't owe me anything. Straight like that but let me help." I knew I could take Sco places, and since I was now a hustler in the sense that my income was based solely on what I could create on my own, it seemed logical that I attack this opportunity full speed ahead. "Ok. Bet," as he nodded his head and smiled. "I'm wit it." We dapped hands and parted ways, and I drove off as Sco's new manager.

After doing research, I learned the best way back then for an artist to get signed was to appear at what is called an artist showcase. At showcases, record industry representatives scout for new artists. After doing a little digging and asking around, I was able to locate an upcoming showcase that was scheduled to be in the South Bronx. I told Sco about the showcase so he could be prepared and waited for the day.

On the day of the showcase, I picked Sco up from the corner of 212th Street and White Plains Road. When he walked up to the car, he had a few of his boys along for support. "I brought my boys with me," he said as he used his thumb to point behind him at the group. I had only heard Sco rap and found out that the others rapped with him as a group. It didn't matter because make no mistake, Sco was the headliner and the one that would get us a record deal if there was one to be had.

We pulled off the block and headed towards the showcase. On the ride there, they twisted up a couple of blunts for us to smoke, on the way. I think at this point rappers and blunts are synonymous, but the good news is there is a belief by many that drugs help stimulate the three sections of your mind responsible for creativity. The location of the showcase was a small club on 163rd Street and Park Avenue. We parked in the parking lot and walked across the half-empty lot into the club. After signing the register, one of the production managers informed us of the ground rules, number one being, "No Cursing." That was definitely going to be a deal breaker for Sco. The contest wasn't permitting profanity because the logic was, if your song ever had a chance to be played on the radio, it couldn't contain curse words. Record executives needed to know that an artist had the ability to actually rap a clean verse. Sco looked a little defeated, but I assumed he was deep in thought. After the production manager left, Sco pulled me to the side and said, "I don't have a song that I can do. Everything has cuss words in it." "Damn," I thought. "So, this isn't going to be as easy, as we thought. How can this kid call himself a rapper and can't spit without cursing?" Calmly, after collecting my thoughts, I looked at Sco and said, "It's cool. We out." We left the showcase after learning a tough lesson without Sco even touching the stage.

Fast forward to the year, 2008. Over the course of my travels, I came in contact with a dude named James, who organized showcases similar to the one that I had taken Sco to years prior. James told me that one of the record industry people that would be in attendance, was a guy that went by the name June Balloon. At that time, June had connections with DJs such a DJ Clue, and the other various New York City DJs. Clue was still one of the hottest DJs on the street, and always delivering talent. My rationale was if we were able to get him to like our music, Sco would finally get the exposure that his music desperately deserved. By now, Sco had plenty of clean music in his catalogue.

It didn't take much persuasion for me to get Sco to perform. He always was more than willing, and always ready to go. The entry fee was one hundred dollars, which we split between the two of us. As his manager, I expected to pay the whole thing, but since we were all thirsty for the same thing, Sco split the entry fee.

On the day of the showcase, I picked up Sco and his right-hand man, "E-Dot." Dot, as he is often referred to, was the Robin to Sco's Batman. They did a lot of duet songs with each other, alternating verses. Dot was talented and could rap also. However, it was always very clear who the headliner was. While we rode from The Bronx to Brooklyn, we picked the song that Sco would perform. I recommended the song titled "I am Hip-Hop." It was a personal favorite of mine because, in the song, Sco took it back to the essence of the craft and displayed his penmanship. Instead of the commercial nursery rhyme garbage that was passing itself off as rap music, Sco's lyrics had a meaning in addition to a catchy flow. We chose the song because we felt that the industry could use a reminder of what real Hip-Hop is all about. When Hip-Hop was first born it was more than just a catchy beat and some simple chant like many of the songs that are hits today.

We pulled up to the venue, and were met by an old friend of mine, Jennifer. Jenny was a Brooklyn Queen that took some time out to come and lend support. When we walked in the spot, I immediately noticed the room was almost full, and it seemed like a decent turn out. There were about one hundred people in the crowd, milling about. I started moving around the room in hopes of networking and getting some more information on the showcase. I met a few other managers and respective artists, but they were in the same position I was in, and it was a competition. Altogether, there were about twenty-five different acts scheduled to perform.

Sco didn't know I had spoken to James before I handed him our registration fee, and he promised that we would get a decent spot to perform. As an artist at an artists' showcase, you want to perform near the beginning. Oftentimes, after certain artists perform, they and their management personnel leave the venue, and the goal is to be seen and heard by as many people as possible. Even if the record industry executives don't like your music, perhaps another manager or performer there will like what they hear. That could lead to collaboration, which prior to meeting and hearing one another, would have never been possible.

We sat as act after act were called to the stage. Hours went by and Sco hadn't been called to perform yet. By the time Sco got on stage, the crowd had thinned down to maybe twenty people, including Dot, myself, and the people that worked the bar and the talent evaluators, who by this point were tipsy from drinking liquor all night and drained from listening to twenty plus acts perform. Jenny had to leave because it was well past one in the morning; it was the middle of the week, a Wednesday to be exact, and most people had to go to work in the morning.

All artist dream of "rocking the crowd." Many times, especially in these instances, the approval of the crowd can sway the mind of a doubting music industry insider. Unfortunately, with no crowd to excite, the true fire of Sco's performance fell upon deaf ears. On the way out, I made sure to find James and let him know we didn't appreciate the spot that we were given to perform. He offered us a sheepish apology and promised the next showcase we registered for, he would guarantee a better spot on the lineup. We never did another one of James' showcases. Whenever future opportunities came up, Sco's response was always, "Rah, I don't mind doing it, but I have to be first, or second or maybe third at the worst to perform."

Rather than depend on battles and word of mouth, for discovery, we went directly to the source. At the time there was a nightly radio show where new artists' material was constantly being "dropped like bombs" on an anxious public. In an attempt to get signed, we drove to the Hot 97 studio where the show was broadcasted live. When the radio host got out of his SUV to go upstairs, Sco yelled from about twenty feet away, "Ayo! Listen to these tracks! I got that fire!"

The radio dude yelled back, "I can't take the CD on the street. Just mail it to the studio!" I wondered why he couldn't take it and give it a listen. Afterwards, I thought I should have just yelled to him that I was from Spanish Harlem "El Barrio," just like he was. Although I didn't know him, perhaps hearing that would have made him pause. It all happened so fast; the thought never crossed my mind. Maybe I wasn't aggressive enough? However, I knew if we believe there is a plan written for us before we're born, then we must trust in things to play out exactly as they are intended to.

We went down there once a week, for about a month straight hoping that perseverance would eventually pay off. I remember the last time we were there and got rejected once again Sco yelled out, "Come on Bro, give me a shot! We are out here baby boy, and we are hungry!"

It's a shame he never gave us a shot because I feel like, if the dude would have just listened to Sco, I was sure he would have pulled some strings to put him onto a deal. Instead, he seemingly channeled his energy into a different up and coming "battle rapper." He managed to get that kid a million-dollar record deal. Unfortunately that artist was never able to make a real splash on commercial radio. The dude had all the talent in the world but at the end of the day, he was just a glorified battle rapper; but I guess that was the other aspect of the industry I didn't know about.

In March 2009, seven years after originally meeting, Sco and I were still kicking it and trying to open doors. We got connected through the hood grapevine with a dude that produced reasonably priced, high quality music videos. In most of the videos being shot in the projects, most of the young rappers liked to be surrounded by a flock of dudes. It is meant to project a harder image, one that is fitting to the narrative of, "I'm in the streets and I got my whole team with me." Normally we didn't do videos for softer, gentler rap songs Sco made. If we were shooting a video, more than likely it's going to be some gangster shit. For whatever reason, the record industry seems to love that brand of rap music. I suppose the prison industrial complex can always use more fuel for the fire.

Most of the video was going to be shot inside the project hallways and roof tops. Before heading in, Candy would provide curbside background music while Sco rapped. After edits, the video was going straight to Youtube. We figured if we could go viral, the labels would beat a path to our door. The end result was the video came out pretty good. The downside was we didn't generate the buzz that we hoped for. There's a lot that goes into getting a viral sensation; at the time, we didn't know. One of the things that always drives it is the money. We knew the song was good and invested in the video production, but never paid for promotion, which was still a foreign concept at the time. To try, and to fail is better than to never have tried at all, and Sco never gave up.

Besides our music-related activities, Sco and I had some adventures. One story that you may find kind of wild took place during the winter of 2003. It's sad when you are forced to realize what some people are willing to do for money. In the hood, if there is almost anything that you are trying to find, just ask an OJ. Chilling with Sco one day, he mentioned to me that he wanted to know where, a whorehouse was at. Prostitution still happened behind closed doors, mostly in unassuming upscale brothels. The clientele in these types of establishments usually consists of businessmen, politicians, even occasional law enforcement agents have been linked to the madame.

The way houses of ill repute in the hood operate is different everywhere. In sections of Queens, private houses are used. These businesses often attempt to blend in, discreetly with the normal families in the neighborhood, as they carry out their illicit trade. Back around 1998, I remember hearing about a "Hoe House" being run out of a spot on 125th Street, near Park Avenue in Harlem. Doing that type of business, on a main strip of real estate like 125th Street, isn't exactly what I would call discreet. Most of the brothels work hard to maintain a low profile, for obvious reasons. The only way you can find one is to spend enough time, in enough different neighborhoods.

The women that work in the Hoe Houses in the hood were typically illegal aliens from Latin America. These women know they aren't supposed to be in the country, so if they were underpaid or say even assaulted, they would be scared to go to the authorities out of fear of deportation. I had a passenger once put me on hold to go to one of these spots so I naturally, as any other curious male would be in this scenario, went inside with them just to see how things operate.

As you enter the apartment, there are normally anywhere between two and six ladies sitting in a room. If a customer, or "John" as they are called in brothel-land, sees a woman that he is interested in, he goes up to the guy that is running the place and pays a sum of cash for a ticket, which is usually an old playing card. The amount of the ticket varies from as little as $23 to as much as $50. The money received is usually split in some sort of disproportionate fashion between the girl and the establishment. The way most of the ladies view it, most of them are going to make a minimum of $100 a day, which is typically a way higher earning potential than it would be in their home countries. It's tragic. It's human trafficking; and in a lot of instances, it seems like the only option for those women. The amount of money these women make is all contingent on their threshold for work.

So, after the "John" receives his ticket, he hands it to the girl of his choice. At that point, the "John" would go into a room with the woman to handle their business. After about twenty to thirty minutes, a knock would come at the door letting them know that it's time to wrap shit up. If the guy wasn't ready to finish, then he would either have to focus and make it happen or buy another ticket which would be good for a second session. I've even heard stories about guys buying two tickets, with plans on fucking more than one woman. That always amazed me, because I always wondered how he planned to do that. Maybe the dude popped a little blue pill or something? After their episode concludes, the "John" leaves, and the girl returns to her spot in the waiting area.

When I told Sco I knew where a Hoe House was, he became excited and chirped, "Wait until I tell my boys! Rah, come through on Thursday, I want you to take me there, and I am sure some of these horny muthafuckas from the projects will want to roll along!" "Okay, bet," I replied. The plan sounded good to me. Chances are if I was taking them there, then I would more than likely be bringing them back. When Thursday night came, I showed up at nine o'clock as we agreed upon a few days earlier. As I pulled up to the pickup location,

Sco was already standing outside with five other dudes, three of whom I was meeting for the first time.

After hopping in the truck Sco said, "Yo Rah, pull up to the avenue so I can grab a bottle from the liquor store and some blunts. Perfect. It was just as I had suspected, and secretly hoped for. This was turning into a hold call. After coming out of the liquor store, Sco climbed back in the car and took the bottle out of the brown paper bag. He handed out blunts to be rolled in the backseat and looked at me with excitement in his eyes and chimed, "Yo just take your time getting to the spot. We wanna get right first." That was music to my ears. They wanted to do a bit of joyriding first, and I was down to get paid. As we rolled along, we smoked a little bit of weed while listening to the Jadakiss. I was fine with it; I love cruising through the city at night; it's the best way to really feel the city.

Since I was taking these dudes back home, I began to estimate the amount of time we were going to be together. I figured between the booze and weed; it would take a couple of hours for them to finish their business once we got to the spot. There was also a good chance there would be people already there, waiting. Sometimes more than one guy will want to fuck the same girl, so he has to wait for the other dudes to finish. I'm sure all of this sounds gross to most people, but that is the nature of the business.

After joyriding for about forty minutes, we arrived at the location. The spot used to be located on Anderson Avenue in The Bronx. It normally would have only taken about fifteen minutes to get there and cost about $10. However, there were blunts to smoke and liquor to drink; due to the depth of this call, the cost would be much more that. I found a parking spot on Anderson Avenue, and the group of us walked up to the building. We took the elevator to the fourth floor, and I knocked on the appropriate door. When it opened, we were greeted by the guy running the place. I didn't know his name, but he immediately recognized me from my visit before with my other dudes. I'm six foot five, and I tend to leave a lasting impression on people.

We exchanged pleasantries, and I explained to him I brought him some business, just as I had told him that I would the last time I was there. When he saw how much money I had bought to his establishment, his eyes lit up. He parted his mouth parted to smile, exposing coffee and cigarette-stained teeth, and through a thick Spanish accent said, "Thank you friend, Thank you. If you ever want a freebie, just come any day, and I will see to it that you get taken care of by one of the ladies." He chuckled and nodded to me as if it was a good gesture. I suppose it was if you think about it. If he charged $50 a person, I just brought him at least $300. While I appreciated the offer, I had no intentions of going back to deal with those chicks. "Thank you. I appreciate it," I sheepishly replied. "I'm gonna grab my boys." I turned around and motioned to Sco that it was cool to proceed. Sco and the boys walked in, I walked out and down to Candy to wait. I welcomed the waiting time with open arms. I was definitely still feeling the effects of the weed that we had smoked on the way over there, and I was high. Time flies when you are high. I sat there, lost in my thoughts for so long I almost lost track of time. About ninety minutes or so had passed when one by one my passengers sauntered back to the Candy, with glazed looks of satisfaction on each of their faces.

The ride back to the Gun Hill Projects was a swift one. We had barely gotten through three tracks of the Jadakiss album, and suddenly we were there. "How much I owe you, Rah?" Sco asked. I thought about it, and even though I could have charged him much more, everyone had a good night. "Give me seventy," I replied. "That's the cost of the two hours... Did y'all niggas enjoy yourselves?" I added with a chuckle. Everybody laughed and started reaching into their pockets for cash. They had no problem chipping in on the ride. Sco handed me the dough and said, "Rah you're like a ghetto tour guide. You know where shit is at! Good looking out my nigga!" he yelled excitably as he exited the vehicle. I had a good night too. If only all calls went as smoothly as this one, life would be sweet.

Sco grew up in the hood. Being raised there, breeds sort of a dog, eat dog mentality. Even family members have been known to do each other dirty. There really is no honor when it comes to the almighty dollar, and even though Sco had dreams of making it as a rapper, he still needed to survive on a day-to-day basis. He already had a couple of children and lived with his sister, so he needed to make money until he was able to hopefully get signed. Sco, like many others looked to illegal narcotics as a way to support himself, so Sco sold crack.

One time, Sco's neighbor, Julia, wanted to buy some coke for her boyfriend who was a drug dealer. I don't know why a drug dealer would need his girl to buy drugs for him, but I guess that's another conversation. Sco told Julia he knew someone that would be able to hook her up with a deal. Eventually, Julia became a passenger of mine and told me this story, and Sco later verified it. So as the story goes, Julia pulled up in a cab to meet the person, and she was instructed to get out of the car. As it turns out, the person she was supposed to be scoring from, planned on robbing her. When she got out of the cab, he pulled out a gun and demanded the $3,000 she was using to buy. Well, upon seeing the weapon, Julia turned tail and took off running down the block. Let it be known, one of the most dangerous things you can do in that situation is turn your back to someone with a gun, but I'm happy to say that he didn't try to shoot her in the back. It was already a bitch-ass move to rob a woman, let alone shoot her in the back as she was trying to get away. When Julia safely made her way back uptown, she went directly to Sco. Sco denied any connection to the botched robbery and told her he had no idea that went down. Later, I found from Sco, he actually did try to set her up to be robbed. That was mind-blowing to me, but I understood it in a sense. They lived in the same building for years, but that didn't necessarily make them friends and there's a fine line between friends and prey.

Sco and I had built a rapport, so he used me when he needed to go re-up. Contrary to many of the stereotypes, everyone that sells drugs doesn't live in a shady, run-down part of town. Sco used to go and see a guy that lived in the Lenox Terrace Apartments located on 135th Street between 5th and Lenox Avenues.

Since construction was completed on the first of Lenox Terrace's six residential buildings in 1958, Lenox Terrace has been home to a plethora of local and national politicians, entertainers and businesspeople. One of the early residents was New York City Congressional Representative, Charles Rangel. Mr. Rangel was an African American who proudly served the Harlem community for over thirty years. Sco's connect was a producer who happened to have his hands on a good powder source. They were from two opposite sides of the spectrum if you asked me. Even though this dude had a nice apartment and a comfortable lifestyle, he still chose to dabble in the street game. I never met him because I always stayed in the truck during the half hour or so that it took to handle business. Whenever Sco called and I was in town, I never hesitated to go pick him up. To this day, I wish I could've gotten him a record deal, I'm sure that would've kept him from resorting to some of the things he did. Nonetheless, our bond is forged on friendship and loyalty, and for that, Sco is one of a kind.

Eventually, I learned taking a call from the base is the equivalent of playing Russian Roulette. I don't enjoy Russian Roulette so much; I even toyed with the idea of only picking up women. I realized that wouldn't work either because if you take a call on "first shout," you don't know who you are picking up. A female could always call the base for her brother or boyfriend, or any dude determined to do wrong if it was their intention. I didn't start Roll with Rah, with the idea of driving around nothing but scoundrels. Over that first summer, I had several normal passengers that I got through the base; it just seemed as though my only repeat customers would turn out to be criminals and gang members. Thankfully, soon all of that, would change.

Chapter 5:
Money Makin'
Manhattan

In my early teen years when I first learned of the nicknames attached the different boroughs of New York City, there was the "Boogie Down" or as some would say, The "Burned Down" Bronx. The latter of the nicknames was earned during the seventies and eighties when slumlords and assholes alike burned down entire buildings, leaving a landscape of charred buildings to litter the borough. "Money Makin'" was the nickname given to the borough of Manhattan. If you were a Harlem native, you were supposed to be more fashionable and carry yourself with the swagger that said so. Harlem has long been recognized as the cultural and fashion mecca for Black America since the 1930s.

Brooklyn was known as "Crooklyn." The name was a play on the often-high levels of crime in the many parts of Brooklyn. It seemed like Brooklyn took violence to a totally different level. In the 80's a crew out of B.K. calling themselves "The Decepticons" were the first ones I heard of running around using hammers as weapons. We called Queens, "Quiet" because we thought that most of Queens was residential or suburban. Many of us held the false belief owning a house made you somehow privileged and spoiled. In the eighties, the Q-borough would earn the more ominous title of "Cop Killer Queens" due to the execution style murder of a police officer seated in his patrol car, who was guarding the house of a witness in an upcoming trial against a drug kingpin. As it turned out, Queens wasn't so quiet after all.

After things got off to a rocky start in The Bronx, I thought that maybe I needed to try my luck in Money Making

Manhattan. My plan was to pass through my old neighborhood to see if I could drum up some business from the cats I knew. Hopefully that would help me avoid some of the bullshit I went through the first couple of months on the job.

It was just after my birthday, in late August, when I pulled up to the barber shop owned and operated by my former barber, Moon. Moon had been my barber since 1994, but at this point I had shaven my head bald and didn't need a barber anymore. I still occasionally passed through to check on Moon, that was my guy. Men spend a lot of time in a barbershop, sometimes getting serviced, sometimes just hanging out. It's almost like our social club. Due to the amount of time spent, in close contact while getting a haircut, we develop strong bonds with our barbers. The shop was pretty busy. I managed to find good parking and pulled Candy up right in front of the shop to show off the new detail job; she was sparkling. It was around four o'clock and I wasn't starting my shift until later in the evening. It was a weekday, so I figured making rounds early would give me a chance to knock out some public relations work with time to make it back up to The Bronx for the peak hours. "Moon, what's up fam? How you been? What's goin on with you?" I asked while I proudly stepped through the shop doors. "I'm good Brotha. I got no complaints. I'm cutting, right?" he laughed, turning off the clippers in his hand and spinning the customer around in the chair to face the mirror. "What's going on with you? It's been a minute. You should let me take that down some," he chuckled again pointing to my bald head.

Joining him in laughter, I responded, "I'm good man. The construction thing washed out a while back, so I'm driving for a car service now. I just started a few months back." "Oh, yeah?" he intriguingly responded. "How's that working out for you?" "You know, it's cool. I'm making money. Every now and again I gotta deal with some crazy shit, but for the most part, it's good. I got these business cards; can I leave some in the shop?" I knew Moon wasn't going to say no. He was all about a young Black man getting money. "Oh yeah? That's no problem at all, just put them on the counter over there," he said, as he tapped his chair for his next customer with his left hand and pointed to the counter across the room with his right. "Thanks, Moon," I said, dapping him and walking the cards across the room. I left a few of my laminated business cards, which I made at home, on the counter, and I was out the door.

The barbershop was on 113th Street and Malcolm X Boulevard. I was headed to The Bronx, and before I could reach 130t Street, my phone rang. I answered the phone, "Hello?" The voice on the other end was unfamiliar. "Yo. You just left the barbershop?" I didn't recognize the phone number, but I did just leave the shop; so I put two and two together. "Yeah, who's this? What's good? What you need?" I responded. "It's Blue. Can you spin back and pick me and my boy up?" he asked. "Yeah, I got you. I'll be right there," I replied. "Give me ten minutes tops." "Cool," he said, and just as quickly he hung up.

When I pulled up to the shop, a slim, brown-skinned dude in his early thirties walked out of the shop and climbed in the front; and a lighter-skinned and much larger guy in his late twenties settled in the back. Blue was the guy in the front seat, and his boy was named Vince. "What's good? Where y'all headed?" I asked. "64th Street and 10th Avenue," Blue said. I knew the intersection. It was smack dab in the heart of midtown Manhattan. Midtown Manhattan is the section of Manhattan that contains attractions like Times Square, Rockefeller Center, 5th Avenue; the world-renowned shopping district is located in Midtown. The reality is, when people say they are coming to visit New York City, they're going to Midtown and not the other boroughs.

Blue and Vince were two street hustlers who lived in the projects in Midtown. Blue got his nickname because he sold the weed strain Blueberry Haze. Naturally, he didn't limit himself, and in addition to selling weed, Blue also sold name brand clothing. I'm not sure how he got his hands on the clothes, he certainly didn't look like a shoplifter. Then again, what's a shoplifter look like if they're stealing designer clothes? Maybe he had a connection with someone that works in a store. Truthfully, it was none of my business and sometimes the less that you know, the better. If I were ever questioned by the authorities and given a lie detector test, I would pass with flying colors because I really don't know the answers.

Randomly, I did know that Blue and Vince also sold Nextel phones that they had shipped to them via UPS. I don't know how they did it, but chances are they were ordering them using stolen credit card numbers. I found about the Nextel hustle because I was a Nextel customer. I remember the first time Blue saw my phone, he looked at me with a sly look and asked, "Yo, how much you pay for that?" The question caught me off guard because I had no idea why he was asking me how much

I paid for my phone. I don't remember the dollar amount I told him, but it prompted him to tell me about his connect just in case I knew anyone in the market for a phone. We never revisited the subject.

A few weeks after first meeting the duo, Vince hired me to take him and two girls from his building to Six Flags Great Adventure in Jackson, New Jersey. Vince told me that it would be okay if I brought a friend along with me.

When the day came for the Great Adventure trip, I showed up with my lifetime best friend, Darren. Darren and I had known each other since we were eight years old. We both liked roller coasters, and definitely deserved a day at Six Flags. Vince came out of the building with two younger looking women, one of them named Vanessa and the other named Mo. Vince was in his late twenties and these girls looked to be in their late teens. In certain environments, it is not unusual for younger females to gravitate to older men; but that doesn't make it cool. Everyone was loaded up in Candy and I was about to pull off when Vince suddenly blurted out, "Rah, I can't go."

Vince had been waiting for a UPS delivery of some phones that hadn't arrived yet. I understood the sentiment, he had money on the way and needed to be there to receive it. "Do me a favor. Just go ahead and take them, and I'll pay you when you get back." At this point, I had known him for a couple of weeks and knew both he and Blue were in the streets getting money; so, I figured, sure why not. "Okay. I got you. I'll hit you when we're on our way back," I casually responded. On the way back from Six Flags, I tried calling Vince to tell him that we were getting close. Every time I called the phone would ring and go to voicemail or not ring at all. I didn't think anything of it because I knew he was in the hood, and probably not going anywhere so; I figured that I would just get the money from him later. Later came and went, and the money Vince owed me never made it to my pocket. A few days after that, I tried calling him and his number was off.

I was still in contact with Blue, who told me that Vince was in Florida on business, and he would be back "soon enough." Although I never received the cash that Vince owed me, I gained something more valuable the day of the trip. The young lady, Vanessa, called me downtown to pick her up one day in September that same year. She was with a few friends and a kid that she was dating, "White boy Joe" also known as "Foe." The way he would explain it, either you were his friend, or you were his Foe. As it turns out, Foe would become my best customer over the next ten plus years.

Despite Vince burning me for my payment, Blue and I were still cool. One time, Blue had run up about a $100 tab and, to pay off his debt, he offered me a Coogi sweater. The retail price for this sweater was over $400, and there was no way I would ever pay that much for a designer sweater, so I jumped at the opportunity. It was only three hours of my time for a high-quality piece of clothing that I would have for a lifetime. Ironically, the sweater was two sizes too big, and I haven't worn it to this day. One day I will pass it along to someone large enough to appreciate it.

Bartering has been around since the dawn of civilization. It was the first real economic system humans developed.

Bartering still happens in the streets, and I'm open to allowing passengers paying off their debt with non-traditional forms of currency. Anything from buying gas with stolen credit cards, to ounces of marijuana can be used as currency and almost anything with some sort of cash value, is acceptable in this underground economy .

Blue was a great passenger because I like simple processes. He sold weed and I smoked weed, which was very convenient for me. Additionally, Blue was originally from The Bronx and that gave me access to other people like his close friend named Petey , that lived on Courtland Avenue and 157th Street. One night that same winter, the three of us went to 2 Cousins, a bar that used to be located on 165th Street near Yankee Stadium. It was small and had all the nuances of a local dive-bar, including the unwritten rule that if you turn your back to the bartender, it meant that you would be buying drinks for everyone at the bar.

After a couple hours of hanging out, we decided it was time to leave. I was facing downhill, parked a few feet from the door. Blue was sitting in the front passenger seat and before we pulled off, he lit one of the many blunts he always seemed to have rolled and ready. We sat and smoked for about ten minutes before putting Candy in gear and pulling off. My passengers regularly smoked weed in the vehicle, so I had gotten into the habit of burning incense to get rid of the smell. As soon as we made the right turn onto Jerome Avenue, a police car pulled behind with his lights flashing. I hadn't been pulled over since that fucked up second day on the job. Luckily for me, the cops pulling us over was not a regular blue and white squad car. Instead, it was an unmarked detective unit. As they approached the vehicle, Petey scrambled to put out the blunt in the ashtray.

"Don't trip. We're lucky," I said calmly. "Detectives don't care about a person smoking a blunt. They didn't make the rank of Detective by arresting and processing people for petty crimes." These cops were often referred to as the "gun boys." The spotlight on the detective's car was shined directly at my sideview mirror, blinding me, and preventing me from seeing the officer's face as he approached the car. One by one, each officer got out of their respective side of the car, and approached Candy on opposite sides, flashlights in hand. In an aggressive and accusatory tone, the officer on the driver side shined his light in the car and asked, "What are you guys doing?" Blue answered, "Nothing officer. We just left the bar and now we're on the way home." "Yeah, and smoking weed!" the other officer added in an equally aggressive tone. "We weren't smoking," chimed Petey, "that's just the smoke from the incense." The officer snipped back, "We don't care about that, and we aren't here for that." Their targets were dudes with guns or large quantities of narcotics. Since we didn't meet the criteria, the three of us were allowed to go on "without hassle" after a brief search of Candy. That wouldn't be the last time I'd get pulled over by " The D Boys" while smoking with passengers. However, knowing what they were all about allowed me to always handle the situation with ease.

With the exception of Blue and Vince, Moon continued to do his best to get me business whenever possible. Specifically, there was one passenger he referred to me who was a part- time caterer. His parents owned a restaurant in Harlem, and he got my number from Moon because he needed a ride out to Queens to deliver food for a wedding. I arrived on time to pick him up. He had a few stops to make before we headed towards Queens, so we wound up arriving at the reception over ninety minutes late. I actually drove a little fast to try and make up for lost time once he told me what time he was actually supposed to be there. In hindsight, maybe that's what caused one of the dishes to spill and stain the fabric on the back of my third-row seat. By the time we arrived at the reception, the people had ordered take out chicken and pizza. Can you imagine how upset the people were when the caterer for their wedding didn't show up with the food on time? To make matters even worse, it was a woman that he knew from his church. I felt awful and it wasn't even my fault. Since the people didn't want the food anymore, he gave me a platter of salmon stuffed with crab meat as token of appreciation. He didn't know I have shellfish allergy, so I couldn't enjoy it; but I remember my fiancée having a feast, when I got home that day .

Moon referred me to one more set of passengers worth mentioning. It was a cool, but not freezing cold December night that same year. My phone rang, and a young voice was on the other end. "I got your number from Warren. We need a ride," said the voice. "I got you. I'll be right over," I answered. I had known Moon for a long time, so I trusted any referral of his.

I picked them up from 120th Street in Harlem. The kid that called me climbed in the front and his boy slide in the back. At first glance, the kids didn't appear to be street thugs or hustlers; they seemed to be just another couple of kids that just wanted to joy ride. However, if there was anything the last couple of months taught me, I learned not to judge a book by its cover. I thought back to the kids I picked up and took to Valentine Avenue. Those two didn't seem like troublemakers until the guy came running towards my truck with the blade raised. I knew I couldn't let that little mishap stop me from getting this money, even if 2000 Valentine was always in the back of my mind.

"We only need like an hour," said the kid in the front. "I need you to stop at the store so I can grab some blunts and shit though. Is that cool?" "Yeah, I got you," I answered. After stopping by the store, we rolled around Harlem for about a half an hour while they smoked. Normally smoking on city streets was a no go, but if you didn't give the cops any reason to stop you, most of the time you can get away with it. With about twenty minutes to go before their hour was up, I asked, "Where y'all getting dropped off at?" "The Bronx," muttered the kid in the back seat. I figured that since we were not too far from the 138thth Street Bridge, I might as well make the turn and start heading that way. When he saw me start to make the turn, the dude in the back seat groaned "Nah, not right now!" That was the liveliest he had been since getting in. So instead of making the left at 135th Street and Madison Avenue to head towards The Bronx, I stayed to the right continuing to Park Avenue, one block east of Madison Avenue.

As I drove down Park Avenue, something in my spirit told me to make a right turn on 131st Street and head back towards the West side so that we could continue to ride aimlessly around the streets of Harlem. They seemed more than happy with no real destination in mind. As we rolled across 131st Street, the kid in the front reached for the volume button and cranked it all the way up. The factory speakers aren't built to sound good at that level, and even if I had a nice sound system, who the fuck did this kid think he was touching my radio. That was unacceptable, and I thought everyone knew that you don't get into someone else's vehicle touching shit. The sudden blare from the increased volume startled me, and I turned my head to yell, "Yo turn that shit down!"

As we neared the corner, I looked up only to realize that the traffic light was out and not working. A split second after that, we were in the intersection being broadsided by a car heading north on Madison Avenue. The impact sent Candy careening onto the sidewalk, with glass shattering and spilling onto the pavement. We managed to slip in between a utility pole and a parked vehicle, and I knew instantly that was divine intervention, as we stopped on the sidewalk just short of the metal gate in front of the apartment building. I knew that if I hit that pole head on my truck would have been totaled, with a small chance that my vehicle could have exploded from something piercing the engine. Ultimately both doors on my driver's side needed to be replaced. The car that hit me was driven by an older gentleman in his early 60s, who had his daughter in the passenger seat. After making sure they were okay, I got on the phone to call the police. My passengers had weed on them, so they paid me for the time already passed and disappeared down 5th Avenue.

I figured I would be able to sue the city because of the broken traffic signal, however, I found out the city is only responsible if they have been notified 24 hours prior to the accident. I suppose the accident was a blessing in disguise. I spent that New Year's Eve with my family instead of in the streets chasing money. Money is a revolving door and will always be there to be pursued. After the year I had, the extra emphasis needed to be spent cherishing what I have and thinking about what was to come.

Chapter 6:
Foe,
The Good Luck Charm

Lucky Charms is a cereal manufactured by General Mills that used a leprechaun for a spokesperson in their commercial. The cereal was coined as "magically delicious" and while there's no proof of leprechauns existing, Foe was very much a real person and equally as magical. As of writing this, I just watched the Independence Day fireworks display from his 27th floor Midtown balcony that overlooks the Hudson River. Foe and I would go on to have countless adventures from the time we met in 2002 to the present.

It was a lazy Thursday night. I was sitting in The Bronx listening to the radio, desperately hoping for a call from the base. My phone rang and there was a sweet, innocent and unfamiliarly familiar voice, on the other end. "Hello, Rah? This is Vanessa, the girl you took to Great Adventure." I knew exactly who she was. She asked if I was available to come to Midtown to pick up her and a few friends. "Sure," I calmly responded. I acted like it was no big deal, but I was excited because money was on the phone.

When she called, I was nowhere near a highway, so I gave her a twenty-minute ETA. Even though she had been in Candy before, this was the first time she had personally called me, so I wanted to make a good impression. The quickest way to get downtown was to find an avenue where the traffic flowed, and which avenue depended on the time of day. I decided to take 5th Avenue down. I entered Manhattan by crossing the 138th Street Bridge, from The Bronx and navigated my way through very little traffic. When I pulled up to the address, I saw four people sitting in front of the building. The building was an old-style Midtown tenement flat which housed eight apartments within its small four-story frame. I recognized Vanessa and her friend from the Great Adventure trip, the two boys I would later find out were named Jose and Foe. The building turned out to be the building that housed Foe's grandmother's apartment. Vanessa pointed to Candy, and the group made their way over and piled in, with Foe getting in the front.

Foe was seventeen years old when we met. He looked white, but he was biracial with half of his roots originating in Ireland, and the rest in a Latin American country. He had a small stature and was about 5'8 and weighed maybe 140 pounds, tops. Foe got in the car, buckled the seatbelt and immediately looked at me and asked, "How much you charge an hour?" "Depends on how many hours, honestly. One or two hours are thirty-five an hour, and once we get to three hours, the rate drops to thirty dollars an hour," I answered. As it turns out, that number was great for Foe. "I'll take two," he responded as if he was placing an order at a deli. They were going up to the Washington Heights section of Upper Manhattan to buy weed, and then they wanted to joy ride while smoking.

In most normal instances, teenagers aren't allowed to smoke in their house, and smoking in the street is not safe because the cops in New York City will definitely bust your balls for it. Usually if a young person has the money to do it, they'd rather ride around and smoke. Word is the best weed in the city comes from The Heights, so they figured they could just kill two birds with one stone; pick up the weed and joyride all at the same time. We drove to 173rd Street, between St.

Nicholas and Amsterdam Avenues. "Pull over by the fire hydrant. I'll be right back," Foe said as he hopped out just as fast as I put it in park. In my experiences, the money man normally sits in the front while sending the flunkies in the back to do the leg work. I later realized that Foe was the man, and after a few minutes, he came back safely with the bud.

Most of the time the most dangerous part of these types of calls is buying the weed and then getting off the block without being pulled over by the police. The cops are sometimes watching the spot, waiting to pull over the customer with a fresh purchase. Typically, cops arrest the buyers and not the dealers because if they arrest enough people coming to buy, the word gets out the block is hot, and people will stop coming to purchase. Foe was either smarter than the average seventeen-year-old, or maybe just experienced enough at his young age to know; so we parked up the block and he walked up.

After Foe copped the bud, we made the usual stop by the bodega. Once we picked up whatever munchies and cigars were needed, we headed three blocks over towards the Westside Highway and merged on. Once we were on the highway safely, the group riding in the backseat started twisting the blunts. In the blink of an eye, weed smoke filled the inside of Candy, as "Many Men" by 50 Cent vibrated through the speakers. We cruised along with the flow of traffic, casually keeping pace as to not arouse suspicion from any other drivers or potential cops. It seemed like it took us five minutes to drive the one hundred plus blocks to Greenwich Village. I know that I wasn't driving fast, not nearly as fast as time moved while I was high. We did a quick loop through the cobblestone streets of The Village, then turned around to head back uptown. I decided to drive through Times Square to see the lights at night and burn some more time before dropping them off. The girls got out at the same projects I picked them up from for the Great Adventure trip.

It seemed strange I had barely heard a word from Foe during the entire time he was in the car. The only thing I remember him saying, outside of asking how much he owed me, was that he wished he had met me during the summer because he calls the base all the time. When we were dropping Vanessa off, he didn't get out to give her a hug or a kiss; and that was when I realized they obviously weren't a couple. Eventually we pulled up to Foe's grandmother's block. "How much I owe you?" he asked. I looked at the clock. It had only been a two-hour hold, but it was an enjoyable experience. "Seventy," I responded. Foe reached into his pocket and unfolded four twenty-dollar bills, "Here's eighty. You cool with me getting your number and calling you directly? I'd rather call you than go through the base." "Yeah. No doubt," I answered. I was more than happy to pass my number on, especially if it was only going to lead to more money. Foe got out of the car, and that ended the first of our many dealings with each other.

The following Wednesday, Foe gave me a call and asked me to pick him up from the same location as before. This time he was by himself, a good thing, because it would give us some time to talk. He climbed in the truck, and simply said, "The Heights." I pulled off and started driving towards the highway with the radio so low, it was basically silent. Something was eating at me from the time that I met the kid, and I couldn't take it anymore. I asked him, "How did you get the name Foe?" "I was pretty good at hockey when I was a kid. In the league I was in, the kids either loved me because I was on their team or hated me because I was their foe on the other team," he answered calmly. "Yo, do you mind putting this in?" he asked as he handed me a CD. I put the CD in the player and recognized the familiar voice of 50 Cent plus his homies in G-Unit. "I'm basically an only child. Like my little sister is six, I'm homeschooled," he trailed off looking out of the passenger window. "Like I don't really have any real friends for real, you know."

I felt for him. As we continued our interactions over time, I noticed Foe had a terrible weed habit and needed to smoke practically every day. We would go uptown, and he would buy enough weed to last him about a day, and then the next day he would have to go back for more. One day on our way uptown I asked him, "Yo. Why don't you buy a large enough quantity to hold you down for a few days? I feel like you spend so much bread running back and forth." "Honestly? If I did that, I'd just sit around and smoke it all day, and the result would be the same," he quipped. "This way is cool; it guarantees I get out the crib. It's not that bad for real." We continued the ride uptown and chilled for two hours. It was almost identical to the first ride we took when he paid me the eighty dollars. The only difference with this trip was the stop at the McDonald's on 34th Street and 10th Avenue before the drop off.

As the depths of winter rolled in, Foe called with more regularity. We continued to go uptown as always and joyride around the city. One night, I decided to take Foe to a strip club instead of riding around aimlessly. My personal belief is every man should experience a strip joint at least once in his life; it's a rite of passage. We left The Heights and headed straight to Wedge Hall in Hunts Point. Wedge Hall was the hole in the wall hood spot that my homeboy, Deezo, spun at. At first, Foe was nervous about being a white boy chilling in the hood. Way before gentrification was the norm, white people in the hood wasn't commonplace and sometimes drew unnecessary attention. Foe, as most white people would have presumed, thought there would be nothing but thugs and hooligans in the club. Honestly, he was mostly right, but I assured him there was nothing for him to worry about.

Society conditions people to believe whatever you are presenting to them. Everyone inside the club was going to see Foe and would recognize he had enough heart to be there — casually sitting and enjoying himself enough to give everyone pause and think twice before engaging him. If he looked as if he didn't have a care in the world, it would signify he belonged and was clearly connected in some way or another.

Foe and I smoked on the way to the club per usual. Security checked us to make sure we weren't strapped. As soon as we walked in, I made my way to the bar to grab us a couple of beers. The pole on the main stage donned a chocolate complexion woman dangling upside down spread eagle. As she gracefully slid down to a shower of dollar bills, we walked over to the DJ's booth so I could introduce Foe to Deezo.

"Yo Deezo," as we dapped, "I want to introduce you to my guy Foe. Foe this is Deezo," I said as I turned to Foe and pointed to Deezo. "What's good?" He gave Foe a fist bump, and quickly went back to selecting records. At any club, the DJ is the most important employee, and strip clubs were no exception. Foe returned the fist bump and turned towards the stage. There was an empty table a few feet away in between the booth and the stage, so we sat in what would be a prime spot to scope the dancers and socialize if any happened to walk by. As the night progressed and Foe became more comfortable, I left him and took a walk to see what the rest of the club had to offer— and even if amusement was my purpose for being there, I never lost sight of my responsibility, Foe. He never left his seat but managed to throw a few dollars on the stage.

While walking around the room I noticed that Foe was getting attention from a few of the ladies who were making their rounds in the club. The women that aren't on stage, are typically chatting dudes up trying to squeeze some extra ducats out of them. For sure, they tried to get him to go in the back for a private dance, which depending on the club, could be a bunch of things ranging from a lap dance to a handjob or even "a quickie". A few guys sitting near him looked like they were probing him to see if he was a target or if he belonged. On the ride over, I told Foe his silence keeps people guessing, and that would be to his advantage. Remember that lesson. Always keep folks guessing.

We spent a couple of hours at the club before we decided to head home. We weren't out of the parking lot before Foe asked, "Can we stop by McDonalds?" After all, he was only eighteen and still had a lot of childish ways. Eighteen-year-olds are still kids even if they are considered legal adults, and Americans get addicted to fast food at an early age, with some never breaking the habit. "Yeah, we can stop. There's a McDonalds just before the highway," I replied. I knew Foe had a good night, but he hadn't actually told me yet. I figured that was exactly the amount of excitement he needed. "You have a good night?" I asked. He smiled "Yeah, it was dope. Thank you. It was good to get out of Midtown to do something besides ride and smoke. It also felt kind of good to be in dangerous spot and to come out in one piece...not to mention the titties," he chuckled.

That night changed Foe. Now when he walked the streets of Midtown, he would have a different swagger about him. Unlike most kids from his neighborhood, Foe had chilled in the hood, the real hood. After being in that environment, walking the comparably tame streets of Midtown Manhattan would be a piece of cake for him I dropped him off knowing full well that we would be linking up again real soon. Most of the kids in Midtown couldn't relate to what Foe had experienced that night. For the most part, the hood they know is the crap they're fed by the media. They nothing about being shoulder to shoulder with real thugs, or even being the only white boy in the room.

One day in the spring of 2003, Foe called me to come pick him up. "Yo Rah, what's good? Can you come get me?" he asked. "Yo. What's up," I responded, "yeah, I got you, it'll be about twenty minutes or so though..." Foe realized that I was doing him a favor as much as he was looking out for me with the cash which was much appreciated. He rarely, if ever, tried to rush me. "No problem. That's fine. Take your time, and I'll see you then," he chimed calmly. "Okay, word. I'll see you in sec. Peace." I hung up the phone quickly and finished getting dressed so I could scoot out the door. Leaving from my crib gave me a bit of a more direct route to Midtown. It was pretty much all highways but would still take me about twenty minutes. Having Foe as a regular, meant that the path to that one hundred dollar a day minimum, would be much easier. I got off the West Side Highway, made the left on 50th Street and pulled up to Foe's grandmother's building as I usually did when I picked him up.

This time, waiting with Foe was another white kid. This little white boy was unlike any other that I had met and to this day have yet to meet. Foe introduced him as simply Red. Unlike Foe, he was a full-blooded white boy. He was one hundred percent Irish and programmed with the Hell's Kitchen mentality. From the mid-1800s to the mid-1980s, the area of Manhattan stretching from 34th Street to 59th Street, and from 8th Avenue to the Hudson River was a very tough neighborhood. While it is now known for its lavish shopping, restaurants and Broadway shows, that charming facade was once an area rich with gangsters and ghosts, streetwalkers/prostitutes, illegal bars, mysterious disappearances, and gruesome murders.

When we met Red's uncle was in jail for murder. The Feds raided their apartment when Red was a child, ransacking the place as they dragged his uncle away. I'm sure he was traumatized from the experience which undoubtedly led to his hatred for cops and authority. Red was not the least bit physically imposing. He stood about five foot seven and weighed maybe one-hundred thirty pounds soaking wet. However, what he lacked in size, he made up for in fortitude, or cojones, as my Spanish friend would say. As we started driving, Red was the first to break the silence. "Yo, it's really nice to meet you Rah," he paused, "Foe's told me a lot about you. You know I appreciate you looking out for him like you do." Red acted as a sort of bodyguard for Foe. "Word. Good to meet you too. That ain't about nothin man, Foe's good people," I replied. "Yeah, he is…that's my boy since we were toddlers," he cheerily responded. "Word up. Say, where we headed?" I loved the small talk and getting to know people, but I was there for money, and we needed to start the trip. "We're still going uptown, but you can take your time. We already got weed," Foe chimed in. I put Candy in gear and pulled off. "Yo seriously, I appreciate you looking after Foe," Red said as he exhaled a large cloud of smoke. "I'm B.L.O.O.D, and I ain't scared to get at any of these punk ass midtown bitches at any given moment." All of this was a little overwhelming. I never imagined that this little white boy would be banging with the B.L.O.O.D.s. I guess gangs are equal opportunity employers .

We were cruising up the Westside Highway listening to Fabolous when we reached the exit at 181st Street. There was plenty of blunt left, which meant there was still plenty of smoke in the air. So instead of going straight as I normally would, I made a right to avoid the red light. There was a stop sign at the next intersection, so I began slowing down and as we got closer to the corner to come to a complete stop. When I looked to my left, I noticed there was a police car sitting there. Foe put the blunt out just in case the cops decided pulled us over. Sure enough as soon as we passed through the intersection, them pigs pulled behind us with those siren and lights, stopping us about twenty - five feet after the corner. As the cop walked up to the window, I began to prepare myself for what should've been a very brief interaction. Also, I was genuinely pissed. "Why did you stop me?" I continued, "I stopped at the stop sign, I couldn't have possible been speeding. So, why'd you stop me, officer?" The psychology behind immediately questioning approaching officers is simple. It puts them on the defensive and gives you a slight upper hand in the situation. Flustered, the officer replied, "You only stopped because you saw us at the corner." Foe and I both let out laughed out loud. "You have to be kidding me," Here's my license and registration." The cops disappeared to their car and returned in less than three minutes handing me my paperwork back while sheepishly saying "Have a good day." They never even made mention of the smell of marijuana which must have been seaping from the vehicle. My line of questioning probably caught him off guard, so he hurriedly wanted to check the paperwork and be done with the situation because he knew the stop was bullshit. The whole time we were pulled over, Red sat in the back silent, not moving, but obviously pissed off. As we drove away, he finally blurted out, "I fucking hate cops!"

We were still headed uptown because Foe needed weed for the following day. Once we copped the bud, it was back downtown we went. We smoked and chilled for a bit more than two hours, and this time I only charged Foe sixty dollars for the time. After all, he was a regular, so I didn't mind giving a break every once in a while. Red grew on me that day as the time progressed. I found him to be a funny kid, and he was like most people that I have come across on the street, tough on the outside, soft on the inside.

One night, as we were finishing up another one of our riding sessions, Red randomly mentioned he played chess. I was always on the lookout for a good match and kept a board in the truck for that very reason. It was about one o'clock in the morning on a Wednesday night, and I had nothing planned after dropping them off; so, I figured we could chill and play a few games before I called it a night.

The parks in New York close at dusk, so sitting in one after hours gives the police more of an excuse to harass someone; and it's not like they needed more of an excuse to fuck with you anyway; stop and frisk was a thing. "Let's go sit by the Trump Towers," Foe suggested. "All that stuff is pretty new still; we should be fine chillin' over there. Also, it's private, so the cops can't say shit unless someone calls—and nobody is gonna call." The towers he was talking about actually looked like a mini city to me, so I started calling it such. Trump City is a collection of high-end, deluxe condominiums that Donald Trump built along the Westside Highway; it stretches from 62nd up to 72nd street with a view of the sunset over the Hudson River. I wasn't sure that was a good idea. As a Black man, I didn't feel that urge to wander onto private property that my passengers shared; but it was his neighborhood, so I trusted his word. "Word. Let's go then," I responded. I grabbed a parking spot and the three of us had a seat on the benches in front of one of the buildings. Over the next two hours, Red lost four or five games of chess, Foe rolled at least three or four blunts while we sat there, and we chilled. The security guard looked every bit of the stereotypical mid-to-late forties and overweight security guard; and could be seen periodically glancing at us. He probably assumed Foe and Red were residents and he never came over to question us or ask us to move, so we left when we were ready.

Somewhere between the fifth game and our exit, I began explaining the advantage that Foe and Red had over me — the white privilege that permitted us to stay well beyond the amount of time that would have been permitted if I was by myself. That is an example of the power that I was explaining to Foe that he had. "You know the only reason we were allowed to stay this late is because both of you are white, right?" I asked them, unprepared for a response, knowing that one wasn't needed because all three of us knew why we were still playing chess at Trump City. I continued, "White people don't know what white privilege is, but Black people do. I think white people do to. It's a power that y'all have that allows you to not even think about whether or not you can be in any space you please. There's no way I could've been here this late if I was by myself, regardless of what the fuck I was doing." "I get it," Foe said as he exhaled a cloud of smoke. "Definitely." "Yeah, me too, yo. White people can be fucked up, sometimes" chimed Red. "There's good and bad in all races my Caucasian brother" , I reminded him.

I drove away that night not thinking about how the words would impact them, I just needed to express what was happening. They understood and they were never the kids that wouldn't get how white privilege existed.

There's a street proverb, "Karma is a bitch with a great fucking memory." Red's gangster ways caught up with him years later. In early 2016, while out of town with another kid from the hood, they tried their hand at a home invasion. Red's homie had a thing going on with some chick out of town, who apparently helped arrange the setup. Her claim was it would be an easy job— the dude they were going to rob was a punk and wouldn't put up a fight. Due to the expected low level of difficulty, they went to rob him with Red carrying a baseball bat and the homie carrying a hunting knife. When they burst into the house, they quickly found out that the homeowner was not only not a punk, but he was a gun owner as well. Red was shot and killed on the spot, while his partner managed to get out of the house. He was later found hiding in the woods by the state police and is currently serving a very lengthy sentence. He was charged with the home invasion, assault, attempted murder of the homeowner and probably a gang of other charges police like to tack onto an arrest, in addition to also being charged with Red's murder.

I guess now is a good time to explain why the title of this chapter is, "Foe--The Good Luck Charm." Foe and I have been in each other's' company around, roughly 300 times. It's almost guaranteed in every single instance, there was some sort of illegal activity going on and neither of us was ever arrested. We have been stopped a few times, and every time the two of us walked away Scott free. One time, we pulled up to buy weed from 173rd Street between St. Nicholas and Broadway. I parked and waited on Broadway at the Chicken Shack, the fried chicken spot, rather than draw attention to the weed spot.

It was nighttime, so it was safe to figure that some of those D-boys were in the area.

Foe hopped out and went around the corner to buy the weed. Less than two minutes later, Foe came walking back around the corner, opened the door and climbed back into Candy. "He's still waiting to re," he said as he blew warmth into his hands. "Re" is short version of the slang for resupply. "That's cool. You want to get some chicken?" I asked. Foe nodded, "Yeah, I'm with that. I could eat for sure." Candy was parked but running, so I turned the engine off. As soon as I stepped out, a brawny officer rushed over to me, and another skinnier officer hurried to Foe. "Alright you two…get the fuck up against the wall," said the skinnier officer. "Spread Eagle!" he shouted. Ordinarily I would have a quip about how the officers addressed us, but this time I figured I'd save it for the end. While the skinnier officer proceeded to pat us down, the brawny officer began making conversation in the form of interrogation. "What are you guys doing out here?" he asked. It was almost as if he expected us to tell him the truth. "Getting some chicken," I replied coolly. "You ever eat here?" I nodded to the Chicken Shack we were being frisked next to. "I love it." "I don't eat that shit," he muttered. "Joe, they clean?" "Yeah," the other officer begrudgingly added, "they're clean."

It's a good thing that the weed man was so popular we were waiting for him and not the other way around. Foe and I turned around to face the officers. "Oh, so we're free to go officers?" I smirked. "Get the hell outta my face", a clearly flustered cop said. We walked into the Chicken Shack to place our orders and had a good laugh while waiting.

After a few too many close encounters in the Heights, Foe decided he should maybe try a new connect. He hit me up one summer afternoon to swing through to get him and a new homegirl of his. Three in the afternoon is actually the perfect time to do anything illegal. For whatever reason it is, cops seem to have a false belief that criminals don't work the day shift and are relaxing during daylight hours .

When I picked them up, Foe climbed in the passenger seat and said, "Yo, this time, don't go to the Heights, go to Inwood." Inwood was infamous in the hood for being home to Post and Vermilyea Avenues, both were blocks with great bud. As we drove uptown, I assumed that we would be going to one of those blocks, but Foe had other ideas, and he directed me to a building on Seaman Avenue. Apparently, he had met a new connect that he wanted to try out. Well, the new connect had us sitting in front of his building for thirty minutes while he took his time doing who knows what upstairs. Foe was turned around talking with his lady friend, when his phone finally rang. "I'll be right back," he said as he scooted out to meet his connect. A few minutes later he returned to the truck, got in, and I pulled off to make the left turn on Dyckman Avenue. As soon as we turned, a detectives' car pulled up behind me with the sirens blaring. Three officers got out of the vehicle; two officers approached Candy, while the third one stayed behind to observe.

"I need everybody to get out and step to the back of the car," said the officer that approached the window first. He was white and everything about him looked like an undercover cop, from his too tight t-shirt down to his Nikes that were

unfashionably laced. Foe opened his car door first for him
and shorty to get out of Candy. The cop on the driver's
side backed away for me to get out. "You don't have to go
anywhere buddy, just stand right here," as he motioned to the
rear quarter panel. "What's goin on? Where ya headed?" I
was kept on the driver's side of the vehicle for questioning,
while Foe and his friend were on the side of the truck. Cops
do this during stops to make sure our stories line up when they
are compared with one another's. As a driver, I learned to never
hold anything illegal on my person. The cop circled his index
finger in a swirling motion, signaling he wanted me to turn
around. I turned to position my back towards him and placed
my hands on Candy's cargo window to prepare for the frisk.
Off to the side I could see the fuzz talking to Foe through the
tinted windows when I felt a firm hand pat my upper thigh, and
then reach into my pockets. "We're headed back downtown,"
I said firmly. "Oh yeah?" the cop sarcastically asked. "What's
downtown?" "The kid's house. Why'd you stop us?" I
retorted. "Because we can. Sit tight, I'll be right back," he
sharply replied before walking around to the other side of
the car.

I overhead the officer who had been patting down Foe say,
"Pat this kid down for me. I think he has weed on him." A
devilish look briefly appeared on the second officer's face then
disappeared. "Oh yeah?" he said as he began to search Foe,
turning his pockets inside out and finally moving on to check
his cap and socks. He still didn't find the weed. "Where's it
at, kid?" As if Foe was really going to tell them the truth. The
third officer who had been watching the whole time, happened
to be a supervisor and decided to get involved. He was large

and musclebound, with the face and demeanor that said he had seen a lot more time on the streets than the two patting us down. It was almost like deja vu watching him go through the same routine with Foe that the other two had previously attempted. Again, the search yielded zero results. Frustrated, the cop took a step back away from Foe with the same look of determination to find the weed as the other two cops. "Where the fuck is the weed?" he asked through his teeth. Foe looked at the cop with the same innocent look in his eyes that he looked at the other two cops with and calmly responded, "I don't have any."

The officer that originally patted me down took three steps towards Foe and began sniffing him like a bloodhound and murmured, "That's bullshit. I can smell it…yeah, I can smell it." As he moved in closer, he began looking Foe up and down. "Where's the bud?" he asked again. Foe manipulated his expression from innocence to incredulous, looked the officer in his eyes and said, "I smell like weed because I just finished smoking…but I don't have any on me now," he smiled. Annoyed and unable to find weed, the officers looked at us in disbelief. "Get the fuck out of here," said the sergeant angrily. "I better not see this fuckin' truck again either." The three of them walked back to their car, and we got in Candy. Obviously, Foe had the weed stashed in a place they couldn't find; I am not sure where it was, nor did I ask. In either case, we drove off giggling all the way downtown, while thinking to ourselves "We did it again."

As Foe got older, his grandmother stopped giving him money, but used her connections in the theatre industry to help land him a job as an usher at the Broadway Theatre's version of "The Lion King." He worked there for a few months, but the hours were inconsistent, and that lead to Foe getting frustrated and quitting. He figured he would be better off finding a way to make money in the streets so he become a small-time drug dealer, starting with selling weed. It was the easiest and most logical choice for him since he smoked all the time and normally had weed on him. In addition to marijuana, Foe got involved in moving small amounts of cocaine throughout the New York metropolitan area. It was no secret he had a weed habit and was used to having hundreds to spend, so he felt like this was the best way to maintain.

He partnered up with his neighborhood friend, Will. They were both around twenty-one when they started their "business" . Will was a slim Puerto Rican kid, no taller than 5'8, with a lot of energy. The first time we met, him and Foe were at Foe's grandmother's house before we headed uptown to the Heights for our usual weed pickup. The exception to this trip was they weren't going to buy forty or even sixty bucks worth of weed per usual. On this trip, they were bringing back an ounce. At the time, an ounce of high-quality Hydro or Haze sold for about $400. The two of them, would go halves on everything to the point, there would be many nights where Foe wanted to go out joy riding, so he would call Will along mainly to split the costs.

I try to have a positive impact on anyone that crosses my path, and Will was no different. Sometimes, I felt an extra need to talk to Will because he was the right hand of my best passenger, and now good friend. As it turned out, I would have had more success reasoning with a brick wall than I did with Will. He didn't seem to pick up a lot of the gems. Most things were either met with a fiery rebuttal or went completely over his head. He was pompous and arrogant, no doubt the result of him being an only child—one whom sharing wasn't a priority, nor was mindfulness or rational thinking when debating anyone. It's easy to be right in your mind when no one is there to challenge your ideas. He had a day job working with his father at the Queensbridge Housing Project in Long Island City on the maintenance crew. Part of their responsibilities included landscaping and with my background as a tree inspector, I figured this would be a good starting point for us to connect. As it turns out, he didn't care.

As a passenger and partner of Foe's, I figured it was in my best interest to ignore the stupidity that would come out of his mouth from time to time. Will and I are also both Virgos , which probably contributed to us not fully understanding each other. If it's one thing that I know about Virgos, we have huge egos and don't like to admit being wrong, until we mature and realize that being wrong doesn't make you stupid. Some folks never come to that understanding within themselves. In full transparency, most of the silly things he said were said when he was under the influence, he wasn't always annoying.

One night, the three of us left The Heights after buying weed and hopped on the FDR Highway headed downtown. We already smoked a blunt on the way to the weed spot and had just made the regular stop at the bodega to pick up some more blunts and brew. When we first got on the highway uptown, we opened the beers for the ride. Foe was already rolling the next blunt. He wanted his usual two hours before getting dropped off, so we rode along at a slow enough pace to make sure we had time to finish smoking before exiting the highway. As we neared the 34th Street exit, I zoned out and decided to get off. It's amazing how differently the same weed can affect multiple people.

Sometimes it's good to act like a tourist in your own town, so I figured a quick spin to see Madison Square Garden and Macy's would be nice. We came around the bend after passing 38th Street, and to our surprise, were facing two police officers standing in the middle of the road at an impromptu check point. We had less than twenty feet to react and hadn't finished smoking yet. Foe quickly outed the blunt in the ash tray and washed it down his throat with a swig of beer. The ounce of weed he had on him was neatly stashed. The blunt would have raised the alarm regardless of if it was out and in the ashtray. If we were ordered out of the vehicle, the boys were definitely going to check the ashtray. As we crept up to the officers, I could still smell weed in the air.

"Good evening gentlemen," said the officer approaching the driver's side. He clicked his flashlight on and shined it in the backseat to Will who was thankfully and surprisingly sleeping, spitting out a gentle snore every few seconds. He then refocused the light on Foe and finally settling on open beer in the cup rest, between the two of us. "I'm guessing that's not empty," he said sternly looking at Foe. "Care to tell me why you got an open beer in the car?" I chimed in, "These guys were out drinking, and they called me to pick them up." "Yeah, and he got there a lot faster than I thought, I had just bought my beer. I wasn't expecting to run into cops. I'm sorry," Foe added. The cop chuckled. Maybe it was the sight of a snoring Will, maybe or he appreciated Foe's candid honesty; maybe it was white privilege or a combination of all three. "I gotta write you a ticket man. Sit tight." He walked over to his partner and grabbed his ticket book out of their squad car and returned. "Let me see your ID bud," he said to Foe. Foe handed the cop his ID, and the cop quickly wrote Foe a ticket for having an open container in the car. He handed Foe the ticket with his ID, tapped the side of the car and said, "You guys have a good night," and walked away.

I never considered acting before that night, but I know I'm a damn good actor because I was high as a kite and the cops couldn't tell. Foe--The Good Luck Charm struck again. When I was about to drop him off Foe said to Will jokingly " we could've gotten locked up and your dumb ass would still been sleeping."

I remember one time the three of us were riding along and listening to a song from my artist, Sco. Foe had mentioned how talented Sco was when Will decided to chime in, "He's not that great. Dead ass, I can rap just as good as him." At this point, Will and I had been around each other for over a year, and he never mentioned that he was a rapper. I was always looking for new talent, and if he was as good as Sco, we could possibly talk about a hot collaboration. I rummaged through my CDs to find instrumentals for him to back up his claim. After about a minute of hearing him, it was clear he had absolutely zero rap talent, and I had to be honest. "You know, you're not good. Like that was bad…like you REALLY can't rap Will." "You don't know what you are talking about," he responded sharply. "I am nice. My name is 'ill Will.' "You know that's the name of Nas's dead homie, right? You can't call yourself 'ill Will' son. Even if you do rap, which you shouldn't, you gotta change your name," I chuckled. "Man, get the fuck outta here, I'm the real 'ill Will.' He's dead son, that means it's me!" he pompously replied. "You know what?" I asked, pausing to look in the review mirror in hopes of catching his eye contact. "Don't quit your day job." Foe, who was snickering throughout the exchange, let out a roar of laughter as he rolled his eyes and looked out the window.

Will was a terrible rapper but a hard worker because, he loved money. In addition to working with his father in Queens, he also had a second job at a place on 43rd Street between 9th and 10th Avenues. This also meant Will spent a lot of time hanging out at the buildings on the corner of 43rd Street and 10th Avenue known as The Towers. The residents of The Towers are an interesting mix of working people and young aspiring hustlers. One of the kids he knew from 43rd Street was a child actor who was able to get decent roles in a few sitcoms through his mother, who was a talent scout. She did a good job of finding him and his brother work. Maybe it was somebody he knew from the block that got him hired, or maybe he saw a help wanted sign in the window on one of his many strolls past the spot. Either way, Will worked there after he left his first job. That connection of his would come in handy for me because I have gotten many free pies and cakes from that place. Say what you want about the kid, but he wasn't lazy, and he always kept dollars in his pocket. As a result, people always wanted to be around him, and he often mistook the attention for friendship.

As time passed, I met several people in the neighborhood, mostly through Foe, and I noticed the way people talked about Will. Typically, I wouldn't read too much into what people said, however in this situation, the way Will's ex girl, Christine, used to talk to him, showed me everything that I needed to know. She was disrespectful as hell. Will knew a lot of people, and even though we were often at odds over silly stuff, Will never hesitated to call me if he knew anyone that needed a ride. There was one instance around the Christmas of 2005, when Will called me and asked me to meet him at the Toys-R-Us that used to be on 46th Street and Broadway. As I pulled up, I saw Will standing on the corner next to another dude, Ersie. Ersie was the actual passenger and had just purchased one of those toy jeeps that are big enough for little children to actually ride in. He needed to take it out to his son who lived in Jersey. That trip to Jersey and back cost Ersie one hundred dollars.

Eventually he would also become a passenger of mine, though it was only for a short time. Ersie lived in the towers on 43rd Street. He was around 28 years old, tall, and clean cut with a mocha complexion and the type of charisma that kept beautiful women drawn to him. One time he called me to take these two women to the airport. When I pulled up, the girls he was with were white. I guess that shouldn't have really surprised me, but it did. The girl that Ersie introduced me to as his girlfriend, turned out to be your typical spoiled princess. Her parents owned a Ferrari dealership on Long Island, and they didn't approve of her relationship with Ersie at all. She had moved out in rebellion and apparently, her and her friend were using drugs heavily at the time. As we drove to the airport that day, they chatted back and forth about getting high on various drugs, some of which I didn't even know were a thing. She was catching a flight to a rehab program in Arizona, which was ironic because they were smoking on the way to the airport. All she kept talking about was how she didn't plan on being in this program long. She was only going in order to get in good with her parents again and regain access to the money tree she was cut off from.

Ersie would go on to call me a few more times. As you probably figured out by now without me telling you, Ersie, like most of my other passengers, sold drugs. There was a time I drove him around to serve a couple of customers and after making rounds, I dropped Ersie off at an exclusive block on Manhattan's Eastside known as Sutton Place. He overpaid me per usual, as he was a great tipper, and got straight into the brand-new Land Rover his new girlfriend owned. My jaw nearly dropped. The base price at the time was about seventy-thousand dollars. Good old Ersie always knew how to find those cash cows.

On a separate occasion, Ersie called me to pick up him and his boy, Brian, from the Eastside. Brian lived in a luxury apartment building on 38th Street and Second Avenue. He was Black, in his early twenties with a mild disposition and gentle manner, which suggested to me he had been raised differently than Ersie and myself. He wasn't the least bit hood. His building was near the United Nations where the real estate is expensive. A one -bedroom apartment can easily cost you over five thousand dollars a month.

After grabbing them from downtown, we headed up to Spanish Harlem aka El Barrio, to scoop up Brian's girlfriend. From there, we headed to get Ersie's girl. Finally, we were off to our final destination, Shea Stadium, in Queens. Shea Stadium is where the New York Mets played before they built their new stadium, Citi-field. On the ride over, the four of them drank the bottle of champagne Ersie randomly pulled out from the cooler bag he wound up leaving in the truck. One of the perks of my job is that passengers always leave shit behind from umbrelas to cd's.

The ride to the stadium was going to take us about a half an hour. Less than five minutes into the ride, Brian who was seated in the passenger seat, started to roll a blunt. At this point in my career, I had gotten out of the habit of smoking with my passengers; it wasn't worth it. However, when Brian opened his ziplock bag and I heard the crack of the first bud; and caught a whiff of the sweet aroma that filled the inside of Candy, I knew he had the good shit. I would skip the garbage weed in a heartbeat but when it came to the good stuff, just pass that right on over her partna. It's a good thing that we didn't have to pass any police checkpoints along the way, because by the time we pulled up to the stadium, there was a heavy cloud floating inside of Candy. As they filtered out of the car the smoke drifted out behind them, we agreed on the pickup time and literally in a puff of smoke they were off to, no doubt continue partying inside the stadium.

On the return trip, Brian and I traded numbers. The customer list was growing again. His first call came a couple of weeks after we met. It was about three in the afternoon, and he was out shopping with his girlfriend. They needed to drop her and her bags off. Apparently, he had been forced to spend more time and probably money than he planned, on her shopping spree and was now sort of pressed for time. Needing to get himself back on track, he let his fingers do the walking by scrolling to my name and dialing. Insert Roll with Rah, to the rescue.

I dropped her off and had him back on his way downtown so fast it seemed like no time had passed at all. We glided down Second Avenue, when Brian, who was typically calm but obviously frustrated by his girlfriend, finally relaxed his shoulders. Sinking deeper into the passenger seat, he casually said, "Yo Rah, you can shoot past my crib on 38th? I gotta run in really quick and then go see some folks. That's cool?" "Yeah, I got you. That's no problem," I replied. Driving for Brian was a pleasure because of his demeanor. There was never any tension or drama with this kid, except for the obvious underlying beef between him and his lady. That was probably just the usual bullshit most relationships go through at one time or another. Brian and I spent about two hours together that day. The time continued to fly because all we did was smoke weed and cruise around Midtown; we made a total of four stops. Each time we stopped, he asked me to park about a block away so that he could walk up and not draw much attention while linking up with whoever. Afterwards he would shuffle back to the truck hop in, and we'd be off again. I was so high; I didn't mind the brief wait between stops, and before

I knew it, we were done and on our way back to his block. I only charged him fifty dollars for the two hours instead of what could have been seventy or eighty. Downtown OJ's usually charge more than we do in the hood. I knew that by giving him a good price, I would be guaranteeing myself a returning customer. My plan worked to perfection.

It was December of 2009. The first semi major snowstorm of the year was set to fall upon New York City. I was at home when my phone abruptly rang. I looked at the caller ID and 'Brian' flashed across the screen. "Peace Bro, Happy Holiday's. What's good?" I cheerfully answered. "What up Bro? Happy Holidays to you. Yo, you think that you could take my girl and her people to the airport?" he asked. I didn't even have to think about it, "Fa Sho, I got you," was the first thing that came out of my mouth. "Bet. Just so you know though, there is a twist…nothing crazy, but I'm just letting you know." I had no idea what the twist could be, and honestly it didn't even really matter at the time. I knew it wasn't going to be nothing wild. By now he had shown that wasn't his style. "Don't worry about it man. Whatever it is, we'll work it out. You're cool with me."

Brian wanted me to pick him and his girl up from his place near the U.N. There was nothing strange about that. From there, they wanted to head to her girlfriends' homegirl spot in The Bronx, and this is where the twist came in. Once there, his shortie wanted to chill and get "lifted" with her girls before their flight. They were about to fly literally and figuratively high. The bird was scheduled to take off at 1 AM. That left

Brian with three hours to burn before dropping them off at the airport.

The snowstorm was starting to pick up a bit. I saw no point in riding around aimlessly. Even though Candy is an SUV, I make it a practice to not drive in bad weather any more than necessary. As we sat quietly outside of Brian's girlfriend's place, we were all mulling over ideas in our heads. "You know, we can go to my grandmother's crib," I suggested. "It's close by, too." The look on his girlfriend's face went from joy to concern. It's typically not normal for a cab driver to invite you to their apartment. However, by this time there was a level of trust that had developed between Brian and me. As she looked at Brian searching his face for clues as to what he was about to say, he flashed a smile and chuckled, "Don't worry, I will be fine." He got out and opened her door and gave her a quick goodbye kiss and we were off.

A few minutes later we quietly shuffled into the dark stillness that was my grandmother's house. Brian previously mentioned he played Chess, so I figured we were going to kick it and maybe play a game. We ultimately decided not to play. We agreed neither of us would want to leave in the middle of a match when his girl called to be picked up, so we sat in the kitchen and chatted the time away. We smoked on the way to drop his girlfriend off, so time flew as Brian and I just sat in the kitchen talking about meaningless things and watching television; and eventually we got the call to complete the last leg of the task.

We went to get the ladies and made the quick twenty - minute drive over the then called Tri Borough Bridge, now named the RFK Memorial Bridge, named after the slain politician, Robert Fitzgerald Kennedy, and dropped them off at La Guardia Airport on time and without incident. A regular cab driver would have been of limited use to Brian that night. Fortunately for him, he wasn't dealing with a regular cab driver; he was rolling with Rah. Even though things went extra smooth, that was the last time Brian would be a passenger of mine. However, it wasn't the last time that I would hear from him. We were cool, and he remembered how well I treated him, so Brian didn't hesitate to call me when he knew someone else that needed to make some moves.

The next dude he sent my way was a Russian, straight from Russia. I mean Russian as in, "I just got to America six months ago Russian" Russian. He spoke with a thick accent, almost identical to those dramatized in video games and movies. Similar to the character Ivan Drago from classic 1985 movie Rocky IV. It was the early spring of 2010, April to be exact, and a few months had passed since Brian and I had spoken. My phone rang. "Yo B. Peace, how you? Long time no speak," I cheerfully greeted him. "Yo Rah! I'm chillin. What's good? Listen, I'm gonna give your number to this Russian guy. Like for real Russian…I don't know when he's gonna call you, but I know he's gonna need a ride, so I'm gonna slide him your math." "Okay, cool. Thanks, I appreciate it," I responded. "That's a good look." "No doubt. I got you," he said quickly. "I'll holla at you later." "Bet. Peace," I said hanging up the phone.

Usually when people give out your number, there's a call that follows shortly after. I had no idea when to expect the call, but about fifteen minutes later, my phone rang again and this time there was a thick European accent on the phone, presumably the Russian. His voice bellowed through the speaker of my phone, and in his thick Russian accent he asked, "How much you charge me to go to Long Island?" "It depends on how long you take. I charge by the hour," I answered. "How much per hour?" Drago asked. "Forty," I quickly chirped back. My prices had gone up a bit. We were going out on the Island, and I had no idea how far and how much gas I would be using. I had to cover myself with a few extra dollars. "Okay," he agreed. "I am in Brighton Beach. You coming now?" I asked, "When does my clock start?" He knew exactly what I meant. I was quite a way away and wasn't about to drive to Brooklyn for a new customer without some type of security. "I am sure you want it to start now. It's okay. Come on," he said. That's all I needed, and just like that I was off on another job that I was sure would pay me at least a hundred cash.

Despite it being a rainy day, I made good time getting there, and reached Drago in under an hour. He lived in a tall apartment building overlooking the Atlantic Ocean. When I pulled up in front of his building, I pulled out my phone to call him. The phone rang three times before he picked up, "Hello?" "Hey, this is Rah. I'm downstairs," I said confidently. "Oh! I'm coming," he said as he hung up. He seemed a bit startled that I had arrived so quickly. Perhaps he thought because we had agreed to start the clock from the moment that I left Harlem; I might take my time in getting to him. Little did he know, taking advantage of folks is not my style.

I was waiting for about ten minutes before a middle aged
and slightly balding, white man in a black leather jacket
appeared at my driver's side door. I rolled down the window
to hear the same accent, "Raheim?" "Yeah," I said with
a head nod. He walked around the front of Candy to the
passenger side, opened the door and climbed inside. "Head
towards the Belt Parkway. I need to make a couple stops;
it'll be a few hours." "That's fine," I replied as I shifted
Candy into gear. Pulling off he then proceeded to give me
turn by turn directions, every word sounding like it was
coming from a Russian GPS. We made stops at about three
different pharmacies that day. Each time, I would sit outside,
while he went in for about five or ten minutes. I had no idea
what he was doing inside and frankly it was none of my
business. While we drove, he talked to me about the former
Brooklyn Nets owner, Mikhail Prokhorov. Drago told me that
Prokhorov, was connected to the Russian president, Vladimir
Putin. It was entirely possible considering how money and
politics are suitors of each other. Politicians will always need
money; the wealthy will always need policies written and one
hand will always wash the other. As we finished our trip and
were pulling back up to his luxury apartment building that
overlooked the beach, he said, "I appreciate you helping me
with everything today. I will call you and pass your number to
my comrades." "No problem...I'm glad I could help you out,"
I responded. "Let me know if you need me again." "Okay,
Goodbye," he said as he slid me $150 and stepping out of
Candy and disappearing inside of his building. I had a feeling
that I would hear from him again one of these days, but that

never happened. I never found out exactly what it was he was doing hopping in and out of those pharmacies.

About a year later, I got a clue. On June 23, 2011, a husband and wife were arrested after the husband shot four people, execution style, inside of a Long Island pharmacy. Apparently, they were going around to different spots try to get their mitts on prescription drugs like OxyContin and Xanax. I'm not sure what happened inside of that pharmacy or why the situation turned into a quadruple homicide. The wife was arrested for driving the getaway car. Their story ended like a fuckin Shakespearean tragedy or something. Was that what Drago was doing that day? Who knows, right? Thankfully, if that was what he was doing, it never turned violent because I had no idea where I was. I can guarantee if I heard gunfire, I definitely wasn't going to sit around waiting to see who was shooting, and I would have found my way home, somehow. Fuck that, I'm not that stupid. Also, never forget, all of this was possible because of my initial encounter with Foe. I met Will because of Foe, and with Will, came Ersie.

Afterwards, I didn't hear anything about Ersie again for about a year, maybe more. One day I heard a story about him being high on something and hiding in a closet at a Midtown Hotel. Then when housekeeping came in to clean the room, he allegedly jumped out the closet and sexually assaulted her. Hearing that dumb shit caught me off guard. That's not the Ersie that I knew.

Through all of this, Foe continued to call me at least three or four times a week for his usual couple of hours. Crusing around the same hoods is boring as a mutha fucka so we decided to start leaving the island of Manhattan. We headed up towards Westchester County, The Bronx, or pretty much anywhere within reason. Sometimes when we were out joyriding, I'd would stop and pick up my younger brother, Kevin. He was about twenty-six the first time he began riding along with us and mentioning him reminds me of couple of wild tales. The first one took place on New Year's Eve 2003.

New Year's Eve is usually a pretty busy day in the car service industry. People are constantly calling the bases with all sorts of plans in mind, so it is not unusual for a driver to make upwards of $300 to $400 if they worked the entire day. Personally, that New Year's Eve was not a good time. My marriage was on the verge of breaking up, and I felt a great deal of stress and personal responsibility. Instead of chasing money, I decided it was more important for me to be in church as the clock struck midnight, signaling the dawn of a new year. "Yo Foe, what's up?" I answered. "Yo Rah, what's good? Can you pick me up tonight?" he asked earnestly. "Yo, so listen, I'm going to church tonight and I won't be working until after I get out," I explained. "I won't be around until after midnight." "That's no problem," he said. "Whenever you get free call me and come down to Midtown to pick us up. It's just me and my two boys." "Okay. I'll call you when I get out and I'm on my way," I replied. "Peace."

I didn't get downtown to get Foe and his friends until a few minutes before 1 AM and the party was already in full affect. On this New Year's Eve, I was picking up Foe and his two boys who I was meeting for the first time, introduced as Johnny and David. They stumbled in Candy carrying a 1.75 litre bottle of

Hennessy. Although the New Year was barely an hour old that big ass bottle was almost half gone.

I pulled off and we were headed on a spin around New York, per usual. We didn't have a set destination, so I decided that we would go up to Harlem to pick up my brother, Kevin. When we arrived at Kev's, Foe and his friends got out to go inside of my brothers building so they could smoke some weed. Normally I would let them blow it down in the truck, but it wasn't a good idea for us to be riding around and smoking on New Year's Eve; there were bound to be checkpoints all over the place. Since there weren't any parking spots, in front of the building, I stayed in the truck. After about twenty minutes, I looked in the passenger sideview mirror and saw Foe speedwalking towards Candy. He jerked open the passenger door gasping for breath and bracing himself with one arm on the frame— finally taking one last deep breath to compose himself and shouted, "Johnny passed out!" "What the fuck do you mean he passed out?" I chuckled. Foe was still breathing heavy, but it was finally a controlled rhythm. He hadn't even gotten in the car yet, and I didn't think he was going to. "Bro, I don't know. We were standing in the staircase smoking... and the kid took a few tokes and...he closed his eyes and... just slumped to the floor." "Well, where is he?" I asked. "Is he still out?" Foe shook his head up and down indicating yes, and pointed over towards the building.

I went over to the building only to see my brother, Kevin, standing over this kid, unconscious in the vestibule between the lobby and the front door. Apparently, they roused him enough to get him to the lobby and through the first doors before he passed out again. The poor kid was lying on the floor with his right arm stiff in the air, almost as if was petrifying. Without thinking, I stood over him and raised my right arm to forty-five-degree angle, pausing briefly before bringing my hand across his face faster than Will Smith slapped Chris Rock at the 2022 Oscar awards. His body didn't respond to the smack. I knew that if the cops came, they were going to start asking questions I wasn't interested in answering. I took two steps back from Johnny, wheeled my body around to face Kevin, calmly said, "I'm out," and started back towards Candy. Foe followed suit, but not Kevin. It felt like a scene out of a movie, where one character gets too messed up, and the friends have to make a pivotal decision on what happens next. Kev screamed "HELL NO !!!!! You're not dying in my lobby" while striking a mighty blow on Johnny's chest. I swear Kev punched life back into that dude. When he regained consciousness, we dropped Johnny and his boy off at Harlem Hospital before speeding away. Of course, the Hennesy stayed with us. They clearly didn't need anything else to drink.

We weaved our way downtown to drop Foe off and stopped to pick up a few passengers on the way back uptown. Kev rode double with me the whole night. Everyone was so desperate for a ride, they didn't care if we were double or not. We stayed out until about 7 AM. I made over $200 that night, and I didn't start working until well after one in the morning. Kev and I went to have breakfast at the famous Harlem spot that has since burned to the ground. It's the same place that was owned by the parents of the dude that hired me for the wedding catering gig in the last chapter. You remember that ? That New Year's Eve was one of the many Foe and I would spend together and just as well, one of many adventures Kevin, Foe, and I would have together.

During that short period of time when Foe was selling weed, he was working with these kids in Bayonne, NJ. Bayonne is near Newark International Airport, and about a half an hour outside of midtown Manhattan. For about six weeks, Foe called me every other day to make the journey from Midtown to the Heights, and then to Bayonne. That part of the trip alone, cost $80. Foe would often still ride for two hours afterwards, bringing the grand total before he would buy us something to eat to $130.

One night in the spring of 2004, Foe called to make the Bayonne round trip as usual. I was with Kevin, who decided to come along for the ride. We picked up Foe, and on our routine trip up to the Heights, Kevin decided he wanted Foe to buy a few ounces for him while he was buying for himself. Foe obliged, and upon his return we were on our way to Jersey. After Foe made his rounds, we ended up detoured and parked next to an empty playground. "That looks like a cop," I muttered as I glanced back and forth between my rear and sideview mirrors. "Where?" Kev said as he peered behind us. "Son, I was thinking the same thing. I noticed them following a little while back. I just thought it wasn't about nothing. " "Yeah, we can go," Foe chimed in. "It's cool. Let's be out." The black Ford Taurus was parked about half a block behind us and when we pulled out of our spot, they pulled out of theirs. Kevin and Foe both still had weed on them, upwards of two ounces, and the stakes were high. We cruised at the speed limit down the street and as we neared the stop sign, I flicked

Candy's left turn signal. Typically, if a cop is following you or trying to spook you, they engage their turn signals at the last minute, or sometimes not at all. We made the left turn, and the cops did the same. We repeated the same exact process at the next corner and true to formation, the cops did the same. "They're still following us, that's crazy," Kevin added as he watched from behind the tinted windows. We turned onto the main boulevard. As I was making the next left turn, I announced, "I'm going to make this next right, and if he still follows me, I am going to hop out of my truck and ask them if there was a problem!" I switched lanes and got ready to turn off. I made the next quick right off of Kennedy Boulevard, pulled Candy over and hopped out the car. Thirty-seconds later the detectives turned around the corner only to find me standing in the middle of the street with my arms stretched wide and elevated in frustration. The cop that was driving cracked his window as they slowly pulled up to me. Obviously agitated, I looked the cops directly in their eyes with the same vitriol and sternly growled, "Why are you following me?"

I had been through enough police harassment in both in New York and New Jersey and was at my limit. It didn't matter that my brother and Foe had weed on them, that was beside the point. The cops had no reason to be following me other than the fact that I was Black and driving a nice truck. Clearly caught off guard, the cop behind the wheel looked at me and sheepishly responded, "We aren't following you." "You aren't following me?" I laughed. "So, you didn't just follow me here from the park, making the same lefts and rights as me?" "Relax buddy, we're just driving," the cop in the passenger seat said behind his smirk. "Yeah OK," I said turning to get back in my truck. We pulled off without any further incidents or interactions with the law that evening. I couldn't tell you what gave me the heart to jump out of my vehicle and confront the cops like that, especially on a mostly empty side street in New Jersey late at night. Anything could have happened to us. In fact, I have yet to do anything as bold or dangerous as that, to date. The next morning, I found out our father died around the same time of that interaction. Depending on your belief, when an elder passes their spirit visits on the way out. Perhaps his spirit had temporarily hopped inside of me, after all, my dad was never one to take any bullshit from anyone. My actions that night surprised even me. That was definitely some shit out of my dad's playbook. Rest in Power Andrew James Wilson.

Eventually, Foe moved from selling weed to selling cocaine. The burden of trying to help his mom pay bills made the decision easy; weed wasn't bringing the type of cash that coke could. He never sold large amounts. He handled mostly small bags worth $50 to $100. Customers were easy enough to find because Midtown was packed with bars, which were packed with people looking to "party." In this grand scheme, Foe partnered up with a dude named Nano.

At the time, Foe was twenty-two years old but looked closer to eighteen. He had no facial hair and a slight frame. I suggested he play the part of a college student and spend time around Columbia University as a way of growing his business. As you might recall, he's not comfortable mingling with strangers, so that wasn't the best option. We have known each other for over ten years, and he still gets eerily quiet around me sometimes. His partner, Nano, however, was quite the opposite.

Foe and Nano knew each other from the neighborhood and grew up together. He was a pudgy twenty-one-year-old Spanish kid, when we met. Nano didn't go very far in school. He dropped out in the eighth grade and decided the streets were his best chance for survival. From there, he became known around the hood as a bit of a tough guy. If somebody owed him money, they couldn't just walk around like it was ok. Some people in the hood will ignore a debt for a while because they know the person. Nano would step to a person and either get his money or get a few teeth. He was even well known by the cops to the point he would ask me not to drive by the precinct on 52nd Street, out of fear the officers would see him and pull us over. I sometimes dismissed it as paranoia since the windows were tinted. But Nano always insisted, and I would usually oblige, because he was a paying customer.

I wouldn't say Foe and Nano were friends before their business dealings with one another. Their relationship started out with Nano using Foe's apartment as a stash spot because he was always getting pat downs by the boys. He fought with his Mom on the regular because of his career choice, and after she kicked him out, Nano rented weekly rooms for a couple of hundred dollars either in The Bronx or in Harlem. It was inconvenient for him to be running back uptown every time a customer called, and he needed something close to Midtown where most of his sales were. That is where Foe came in and a stash spot became a partnership.

If he was uptown and got a call, Nano would have to make his way downtown. Sometimes, he would take the train but that didn't work out too well because he had customers waiting, and MTA is unreliable, especially at night. That's where I came in and after a while, paying me proved too costly, so Nano would just have Foe make the delivery. Most of the drop offs were close enough for Foe to walk to, and for the ones that required a ride, you already know, it was Rah to the rescue.

Basically, Foe was working for Nano, but after some time, Foe started to build his own clientele. One of his first customers was a dominatrix he met in Midtown who liked to do coke before or sometimes during her dates. The first time I met her, Foe and I were waiting on the corner of 48th Street and 8th Avenue, when an average looking white woman in her early forties approached. She definitely wasn't ugly, but far from gorgeous with very average features. After climbing in the truck to deal with Foe, she mentioned she was headed downtown to meet up with some trick, so we offered to drop her off. During the ride, I noticed there was something strange about her presence that made her memorable. Since I knew what she did for a living, it could've just been my mind imagining her in a sexy leather outfit. Don't forget the heels. I hoped she could become one of my regulars. Unfortunately, that never happened. I actually never saw her again after that night. Most of the times she needed to hook up with Foe, she was in Midtown, often times well within walking distance. Whenever she was out of range, Foe and I were back to doing what we normally do.

There was one time in 2007, she called for a delivery in Queens. Again, this was before turn-by-turn directions were in the palm of your hand using your smartphone. Small GPS units like the Garmin Nuvi had recently hit the market, but I hadn't come out of my pocket for one yet. The five-borough map I kept with me had been torn and tattered from years of use. Without that or a GPS, the trip became a twisting adventure, that took about twice as long as it should have. Queens is just a different fucking borough. You have to visit in order to really understand how confusing things can be out there. It didn't really matter. Since Foe and I spent hours cruising on a regular basis; we were used to being around one another. She was busy with her customer. It's not like she was going to go anywhere else to get her order filled. We eventually found her. A few minutes later we were on our way back to Midtown. Time was spent but I couldn't pass the cost along to Foe for us getting lost. He is a person that I considered a friend. I'm not in the habit, of taking advantage of people, especially not one of my boys.

Foe only had one other customer that I actually remember not coming from Nano. There was an older guy in his late 60s that managed a top steakhouse in the area. Despite his advanced age he regularly copped work from Foe. I guess you're never too old to party, right? Anyway, the gent was a real nice guy. One night we swung through to serve him. Before getting out of Candy he said that we were welcome to stop by the restaurant for a meal anytime we pleased. We didn't get to take him up on his offer, because a few months later, he fucking retired. Dude didn't tell us that the deal would expire like a coupon. The moral of the story is that if someone offers you something and you're really interested, DON'T hesitate to take advantage. Other than those two, everyone else, came through Nano.

Foe was new to the coke business, while Nano had been in it for years and had customers from all walks of life. There was a guy who was a software engineer and worked downtown near Water Street, a short walk from the South Street Seaport and Ground Zero. Apparently, he freelanced for various companies, and made serious bank doing it. I've personally seen him spend hundreds maybe even thousands of dollars with Nano. Nano told me stories about this guy taking him to different happy hours filled with beautiful women and the money-making Wall Street types who were blowing money like it grew on trees. The guy flew in and out of town for business regularly, making sure to always stop and see Nano before taking to the skies. What's this thing with people wanting to " fly high" ? Nano didn't look like he could blend in this guy's circle. I have no idea how the two hooked up. Usually with an "odd couple" like that, one of the people is almost always a drug dealer. The engineer was one of the many functional fiends in society, whose habits in turn, feed millions across the globe.

Much like myself, Nano had a few regulars that kept him afloat. One of my favorite custies of his lived across Hudson River in New Jersey. About half a mile south of the Holland Tunnel sat a housing complex built once again by our 45th President Donald J Trump. I still can't believe that happened. Full of luxury condominiums located right on the water, some of the units sold for well over a million dollars. Imagine having access to so much cash that, you're willing to pay that much to live in a fancy apartment without, having ownership of the land it sits on. For most people that will never be anything more than a fantasy.

It normally took us about twenty minutes to get there from where I usually picked Nano up in Midtown. The entire trip would take us less than an hour. I would still get paid $50 every time. We did that at least twice a week, which meant I was able to fill Candy up for less money, because gas was cheaper in Jersey. Nano kept serving that guy. I was making about $400 per month from his trips to that one customer. Nano also had his own version of Foe, a custie who had proven to be very consistent. I'm sure the guy had some serious paper because that's the only way someone could afford live in a hotel in Midtown. Not to mention the amount of bread he spent on blow. He told me the guy was originally his uncle's customer who he stole away for his deep pockets. I honestly think his uncle let Nano have the dude as a way of getting him set up in the business. That happened when Nano was fifteen and twelve years later, he was still serving the guy.

I'm mostly retired from the business, so Foe and Nano had to start making other arrangements for their transactions. Remember, one of the reasons Foe became a partner is because a lot of their customers were in the area. Foe owned a dog named Midnight. When some of their clientele who lived outside of the area drove down to see them, he would coincidentally be walking him by the park across the street from his Mom's place. No one ever suspected that Foe was doing deals. "Walking the dog" worked every time. Things were a little different when they had to go see their customers.

Nano had street homies that would occasionally let him borrow a car when he needed to make a move. Foe was also always quick to get behind the wheel of any car. When I started driving him back in 2002, Foe was only a seventeen-year-old kid with a love for three things: smoking weed, listening to music, and riding in cars. He loved that feeling of whizzing along the open roads. He couldn't wait to get his hands on his driver's license. That's kinda strange in New York because of the relatively dependable mass transit and lack of parking. Most native New Yorkers weren't and still aren't in a hurry to get behind the wheel.

Over the years, I've seen Foe driving a bunch of different cars. A lot of his customers, as I told you owned a vehicle, and Foe would sometimes trade his work for the use of their auto. For a few hundred dollars' worth of coke, a person was willing to hand over the keys for someone else to drive, with minimal liability. That is crazy. I will never understand the rationale. "That white girl" makes men and women do strange things. Cocaine, cocaine.

Whenever the police started asking around, or he got a funny feeling, Nano flew down to Florida to chill with his boys in Miami for a few months until the heat was off. My understanding was life in Miami was good for Nano's homeboys, and one of them managed a popular nightclub which gave them access to some of the baddest broads in town. Nano never hesitated to show me pictures of the "good life" he lived out of town. Despite the great time, it would come to an end with my phone ringing and Nano's voice saying, "Rah, come get me from the airport."

The strangest things would happen when we would least expect it. The call would start out as a typical run over to Jersey to check his people in Bayonne and then back to Midtown. Spring was in the air and the streets were alive and bustling with the energy that the new season brings. Around 1:30 AM, Foe and I had just come through the Holland Tunnel and were headed uptown on the Westside Highway. My plan was to drop Foe off at his house and then be on my way. Foe always had the option to joyride for free, but tonight wasn't meant to be one of those nights. Tonight was Saturday, which meant that there was plenty of money to be made. We were heading north on the West side, somewhere near 17thStreet, when Foe, face practically pressed against the glass, tapped my shoulder and exclaimed, "Yo Rah, look at those chicks on the corner!" My first thought was that he was pointing out another group of scantily clad women, instead I looked over and saw a group of Black women standing on the corner with one, sitting on the sidewalk. There was five of them in total, including the one seated, likely varying in ages from twenty-five to mid-forties. I managed to glance over in time to see a kick fly towards the woman seated while the others just stood there, watching. I felt compelled to pull over to play peacemaker. I found the safest space to double park as close to the curb as possible, "What's the problem ladies? What's going on?"

The women were taken aback by my presence. A six foot five, two-hundred-and-thirty-pound man can be an imposing figure. My need to intervene was driven in part by the racial makeup of the group. Black people are stereotyped as wild, threatening, and unruly through various media outlets. The last thing I wanted to see was for the group of sisters on the corner to contribute to the negative narrative. These were grown-ass women dressed for a night on the town. One of the women, who we learned was the oldest, spoke, "Those are my little sisters," pointing to the one on the curb. "She's just really drunk. We got kicked out the last cab because she threw up in it." "Bitch, your dumb ass always getting too fuckin' drunk!" shouted the sister as she threw another kick in frustration. "I...I'm sorry," slurred the sister who was sitting doubled over on the curb, "I...I didn't mean to." I could tell that she meant that. The booze probably crept up on her; I had seen it so many times before. "Nothing ruins a night quicker," I quipped. Reaching for one of my business cards, I handed it to the older sister saying "Look, I'm not a pervert or anything, I'm a legitimate driver, and I can give y'all a ride home if you need it."

A brief silence fell over the crowd as they looked at Candy tinted windows as she sparkled under the street light. They had no idea how many people might be in my truck; all they could see was the white boy sitting in the front. In my eyes, it was just as much of a gamble for me, considering she just got done throwing up. "That would be perfect. Thank you so much," said the oldest sister, and with little hesitation the ladies filed into the truck. Foe instinctively moved to the third row, allowing the ladies to occupy the first two, with the oldest climbing into the front passenger seat. I was sure to place the sick woman by the window just in case she felt the need to vomit again. Their original destination was about a mile away, but after the vomiting, their plans were scrapped, and the rest was history. Now they simply wanted to be dropped off and put the whole affair behind them. Thanks to New York City traffic, we had a few moments to get to know each other. I was surprised to find out that a few of the women lived in The Poconos and they were in New York, visiting family—further escalating the frustration with the vomiting sister, as they didn't get to hang out often and the night was supposed to be special. I had recently migrated to The Poconos as well. "Y'all should give me a call since we're all from New York and relatively new to Pennsylvania. We should keep in touch with each other, you never can have too many friends on the side of the mountain," I suggested.

The trip to the projects just north of Houston Street took a half an hour on the FDR drive. Thankfully, we made it there without any further incidents from the drunkard. "How much I owe you?" asked the eldest sister, looking down to search the contents of her opened bag. "Y'all don't owe me anything. I just wanted to make sure y'all were okay. It wouldn't be right for me to just pass by, seeing what was going on, and just keep it moving," I replied. The explanation was genuine, although I would be lying if I said part of me wasn't trying to curry favor with those ladies, in the hope of getting to know them better in the future. I didn't stop because they were attractive, but once I saw what I was dealing with, I may or may not have kicked the charm up a notch or two. "Thank you," said the group as a collective as they stepped down from Candy.

I made a right and headed towards Greenwich Village. "I'm gonna roll a blunt," said Foe. It made sense to cruise around, smoke and kick it, about the wild shit we just went through. I was pulling up to Foe's spot when a call came across the airwaves, "Base time is now 4:10 in the AM. I need a downtown, 54th and 8th coming up." That was perfect for me. The call was three blocks away from where I was dropping Foe off. There was no need to wait for "second or third shout," I keyed my microphone and was made a positive for the pickup right away. About five minutes later, I double parked in front a building to wait for whoever was about to pay me to drop them off on my way home. I was going uptown, and they were going uptown; I loved to end my nights like this. I keyed up on "first shout," so I had no idea who or what to expect. Suddenly the door of the building shot open with a loud metal thud, and a wry smile cracked across my face as one guy made his way out of building, with two women in tow. It was clear from the staggered stumble towards Candy, the women were twisted. They barely looked old enough to drink, and even if they weren't, that wasn't going to stop their party. As they approached, the guy walked straight to the driver's side and said, "How much to take them uptown? Yo! Tell him where y'all are going." One of the women perked up in her seat and asked, "Do you know where Burnside is?" Burnside was less than a mile away from where I used to live, on Morris. Of course, I knew where it was, and even though I was headed in that direction, they still got hit like a regular fare. I nodded my head, and turned to the guy, "That's thirty." "No problem, chief," he reached into his pocket, pulled out a wad of cash and peeled off two 20's. "Keep the change." The girls were already inside by the time I pocketed the cash. Just that fast we were on our way. It was about a twenty-minute ride, straight up the Westside Highway, to their block if we didn't hit traffic. On the ride up, they excitedly chatted about just being in the studio with some new big-time rapper . Traffic was surprisingly light for a Saturday night. As I drove them up the block, I noticed the girl sitting in the rear passenger seat fumbling around with something. I glanced into the rearview mirror to see she was ruffling through a small purse, one that obviously didn't belong to her. If she had quietly picked up the purse and gotten out, I wouldn't have known. Instead, perhaps because she was drunk and not thinking but clearly, she had drawn my attention. Without a second thought, keeping my left hand on the steering wheel, I reached my right arm into the back seat, and snatched the bag from her clutches. "Give me that! That's not yours…what's wrong with you?" Neither of them said anything, as they looked at me and quicky slid out of Candy.

I got back to Granny's and checked the bag to find an ID. The bag had to belong to one of the sisters from earlier, probably the drunkest one. Or it belonged to one of the others who probably was so busy getting the drunk one out of the truck that she left her own bag. Inside of the bag was a wallet with $50, her driver's license, a few credit cards and various feminine items. I realized afterwards, even if I knew to whom the bag belonged, I had no way of getting in touch with them to return it. There is nothing I could do about that right now; it was after 5 AM, and I needed sleep.

Roughly five hours later I was shaken from my slumber by the sound of my cell phone ringing. Groggily, I answered, "Hell..Hello?" A woman's voice came through the earpiece, sweet but clearly anxious, "Hello Rah? Yeah, I was in your truck last night, with the group of sisters…did you find a pocketbook?" The word pocketbook rang repeatedly in my head. I replied still half asleep, "Yeah…yeah, I found it. I got no problem bringing it down to you, I can't do it right now though." "That's fine, it sounds like you were sleeping anyway. Let me know when you can meet me, okay? Thank you, I appreciate it." "That's no problem I got you," I replied. She hung up, and I laid back down. It was three in the afternoon when I decided to make the twenty-minute drive down the highway to meet her. It really couldn't have been more convenient for me. The FDR was right behind Granny's spot on 5th Avenue and before leaving, I decided to keep the fifty dollars cash. When a person loses their wallet, I think the most important thing they would want back is the identification and credit cards. The woman was overjoyed, but she was clearly unappreciative of the gesture. She didn't even offer to pay for me coming down. It's a good thing I took that $50. I had given them a free ride the night before. The least she could have done was offer me something for all of my trouble. Did they forget that I was a car service? I could have easily been grimy and gone on a shopping spree or at least gotten myself a tank of gas before returning her credit cards, but that isn't my nature. I honestly wished that I wasn't so strapped for cash at the time, or I wouldn't have taken the $50.

It was a Saturday night and Foe and I were out for his typical session. On this trip, he brought an unusually quiet Will with him to split the cost of the ride. We were about an hour and a half into the trip when my phone rang. "Hello?" I answered. I was greeted by a sweet melodic voice, bearing all the signs of fatigue from a good time. Patty asked, "Hey Rah, you available?" Technically, and under normal circumstances, the answer was no if I already had passengers in the truck. However, Foe and Will weren't normal customers, and these certainly weren't normal circumstances; I knew that they wouldn't mind if I got a little side money. Where are you?" I asked. "Me and my homegirl just got out of this club, downtown. Would you be able to swing through to get us?" "Sure , the only catch is I've got two dudes with me. We're almost done. I can come get y'all. Then we can drop them off in midtown on the way back up. I can be there in like ten minutes." "That's cool. See you in a few." Just like that, Patty was off the phone.

The closer we got, Will began to liven up. Either he was extremely high and just now coming back to Earth, or the idea of us picking up a couple of females had caused him to perk up; in any event, he suddenly became much chattier. I chalked his sudden burst of energy up to his probable false hope that he would be able to "holla at" one of them. I knew that neither Patty nor her sister-in-law would be interested Will's immature bullshit. When we pulled up to The Spot, the ladies were already standing out front. Both of them, though stunningly dressed, wore weary looks on their faces. The ladies climbed into the second row of Candy, with Patty sliding to the middle seat, and her sister-in-law sitting behind me. I would had made Will move to the third row, but they were getting dropped off next, so that made no sense. After we pulled off, I locked eyes with Patty in the rearview mirror and asked, "What's wrong?" She smiled, "Nothing Rah, I am just kind of tired." "Word. Well, I'll get you right to the crib as soon as I drop them off," I smiled back. I could tell that was some of the best news she's heard all night as we settled in for the ride uptown.

This is where things took a left turn. We were listening to Hot 97; I don't remember what song came on, but the conversation got heated when Will tried to justify using disrespectful language towards women. "I mean, some bitches be bitches," he snarked. "If you a bitch, I just gotta call it what it is. It's not all women, but it's most of y'all." That's offensive as hell. He hasn't lived enough to say some dumb shit like that. While stumbling over his words, trying to explain himself, Will only made things worse. I'm almost positive he was trying to compliment them, but instead wound up on the brink of an argument. I remember thinking, "Only this fool right here could turn a simple scenario into such a mess for no reason." Foe, who had been sitting quietly in the passenger seat, looked at me and shook his head as Will continued on babbling. At one point during his explanation, I even heard Will say something that could sounded racist although though I'm pretty sure he's not a racist kid. Does he sometimes an asshole ? YES. But if he was a racist prick he would never be rolling with Rah. I wouldn't give a fuck how much money he had.

Patty was sexy, from the projects and by no means a lightweight. She had a sturdy frame. Standing around five foot seven, with thick, juicy hips and thighs, I nicknamed her Patty with the fatty for obvious reasons. Her combination of attitude and body made her somebody you didn't want to piss off. Patty and Will went back and forth for a while, with Will digging himself deeper and deeper with every word. It was pretty clear that Patty had heard just about enough. She slid forward in her seat, closed her eyes, and took a deep breath. Will kept rambling, completely uncaring about Patty's change in demeanor. Finally, Patty curled up the sides of her mouth, looked at Will with fire in her eyes and said, "Say another motherfucking word, and I am going to punch you in your mouth!" Will's face dropped in shock as if he wasn't sure how to respond. "That is not going to happen," he mumbled. Patty slowly nodding her head retorted, "Keep fucking talking and see!" She was from the projects, but also was a professional woman who had a Bachelor's degree and was working on her Master's in Psychology at the time. She wasn't some hood rat that walked around cursing and fighting, regularly. However, she never forgot where she came from, and that night all that education didn't matter. She was sure enough bout to punch Will in his fucking mouth. "Patty don't even pay him any mind, sis. He's just fucked up that's all. Don't even trip… seriously," I chimed in from the front seat. I couldn't stay quiet and let things continue to spiral. Divine timing had it so when I was saying that, we were pulling up to Will's Mother's building. To this day, I don't think he realizes how serious that situation was. I don't know if Will learned a lesson that day, but that ride taught me that I can't always mix my fares together. Some people know how to act, and some people don't. After dropping the boys off, I continued on my journey to take Patty and her sister-in-law home. On the way uptown, I remember Patty saying, "That clown needs to watch his damn mouth…if I was a dude, he would have gotten his ass kicked." She was absolutely right, but also sadly enough, if she was a dude, he probably wouldn't have acted like that.

The idea of Foe staying with me until I caught my next call wasn't anything that he or I planned. We noticed more times than not, either my cell phone or the base would wind up putting some money in my pocket while we were together. I am a superstitious dude. If a certain thing or trend works, I stick with it.

Back in 1998, when I first started in the business with the Blue Expedition, my homeboy, Rodney, told me if I wanted to make money, I had to use a certain can of aerosol spray. The spray came in a purple can with an Indian head on the label, with the words money and house blessings written on the can. At first I thought the idea of a spray can to somehow bring myself more money was pure foolishness, but as time wore on, I noticed a strange connection between the two. There were only a couple of stores I knew of that carried the spray. Usually, I got it at the carwash where Rodney had first shown it to me. By chance, if I ran out of spray, I would typically go without it. However, true to what my boy had said, my money was slower during those periods. There were times when I tried to substitute the purple can with a different color, made by the same company. The cash flow wasn't the same.

As I've gotten older and more mature, I've learned there are energies and spirits we can't tangibly see or touch, that are very real. Ancient religions burned certain incense and resins to help raise the vibrations of the atmosphere and environment they were working in. Ancient Egyptians believed that scented oils had the ability to keep evil spirits away.

Perhaps, Foe and I chilling together created such a harmonious bond from which good fortune flowed as a result.

I was like a big brother to him, who's nurturing and teaching during our time together had shown him the highways he would one day navigate back and forth, as I once did. The things I taught Foe all came from a genuine place and Foe could have called anyone for a ride, but he always rolled with Rah. Universal law is you get back what you put out. I always threw love out to others, so it's only right that the universe threw some back to me, which usually happened in the form of a call.

We were out for our usual joyride one night back in May 2004, when I said to Foe "Since we're just driving around gawking at chicks, why don't we just park where they are?" New York City was full of beautiful women, but even more so on the weekend when they seem to head out in droves, to "let their hair down". Ranging in an assortment of shapes and sizes, you can almost take your pick of lassies out to have a good time. Needless-to-say, if you were trying to snatch up one of these joints, the first place you should probably check was the nightclub; it would be nearly impossible to miss the procession. Our trips across the city gave us several spots to choose from, so I decided that it would be best to park up on a block with more than one club on it to increase the amount of eye candy. This part of town used to house a lot of factories during New York's industrial past. Once the factory jobs moved away, these huge spaces went unoccupied for decades until someone got the brilliant idea to turn them into nightclubs. We parked on 26th Street between Tenth and Eleventh Avenues; there were three or four clubs in a one square block area.

The unofficial plan was to park and probably smoke a blunt while enjoying the parade of women walking by, so the best place for us to stay low-key was further in on the block; it was approaching 3 AM when we pulled up. We had driven through a few times but never actually stopped. Even at this late hour, the streets were packed, with no shortage "dimes" strutting back and forth. It seemed to be a representation of every race on Earth. Everywhere we looked there was a sexy-ass Asian chick or a beautiful blonde. I remember this one middle eastern looking sister that was amazing. I was hoping the environment would help drag my boy Foe out of his shell. Being the introvert he was , Foe seemed equally content just listening to the DJ spin on the radio station and staring while we smoked our last blunt of the night.

There was a drunk woman having a terrible time walking up the block. Her awkward stumbling, swaying, and untimely fall immediately caused Foe and I to erupt in laughter which lasted for a few minutes after she embarrassingly picked herself up and scurried along. The last few chuckles had just subsided when a call from base crackled through the radio. As fate would have it, we were parked on the block the call was coming from. I wanted to key up on "first shout," but ass you know it was against base rules for us to ride double with a male. There was no way I could drop him off and be back to get the call in the five minutes allowed for "first shout." The radio fell silent. Perfect! There were no other units in the area. The B1 interrupted the silence again, "Base time is now four oh five, I need a downtown 26th and Tenth…" I keyed up and cut the B1 off before she could even finish her sentence. I was so sure I'd get the call; I was already driving the one mile back to Foe's house to drop him off. The B1's voice shot back at me, "How long, 99?" "Five minutes," I answered quickly before dropping my microphone. By this time, I was already on 38th Street heading up Tenth Avenue with nothing but green lights in front of me. By the time the B1 hit me back letting me know that I was a positive, we were already ten blocks from Foe's crib, I made it back down to the club in plenty of time.

I was honestly expecting someone drunk to come stumbling towards Candy. I was more than pleased my passenger turned out to be just a weary bartender on her way home from her work. She was a Spanish chick in her mid-to-late twenties who, even though tired—didn't mind talking basically the whole trip uptown. I hate the uneasy feeling silent rides often bring. The conversation was much more memorable than her name, which as of now I can't recall. During the ride uptown, she mentioned bartending was her second job, and during the day, she worked as a sales associate at the Foot Locker. She was clearly a hard worker because after her shift at Foot Locker, she would often head straight to the club. With adult responsibilities you do shit like that. I understood why she was so tired. Hats off to all the hard-working folks out there reading this. For some reason I started talking about the New York Yankees. Maybe it was something we heard on the radio. Back then, I was still a huge fan, and mentioned, my love for them to which she replied, "My boss said he is giving me some tickets tomorrow, and I don't even like baseball, so If he gives them to me, I'll call you." We made it all the way up to The Bronx in no time flat. Since it was such a quick ride, I only charged her $20—about $10 short of the proper fare. I am a huge believer in Karma and don't mind "paying forward" because, when it comes back around to you, it's often much sweeter.

I gave her my number just in case she ever needed a cab. Never in my wildest dreams did I think that she would come through with the tickets, but true to her word, two days later my phone rang and she said, "Hi Rah. It's me the girl from Saturday night, you remember; the bartender that works at Foot Locker." "Oh hey, yeah...what's up?" I replied. "Are you busy?" She asked. "Nah...I'm available. What do you need?" I asked. She said, "Cool. Come and get me from my job. Oh, by the way, I have those tickets for you." Both of those things were great news to me. In addition to her putting some money in my pocket, she was giving me free tickets to the baseball game. It took me about forty minutes to get to her job even though I was already in Manhattan. The time of evening left me dealing with a little bit of traffic on the way down to her. One of the reasons I always preferred people calling my phone as opposed to catching calls from the base was because I normally wouldn't get the chance to run a customer a half an hour waiting time. As I pulled up to the Foot Locker, she was standing out front and in much better spirits. She climbed into Candy, and we were on our way. She wasn't in a rush to get home and didn't mind the stop and go traffic on Madison Avenue as we made our way uptown. About five minutes into the ride, she reached into her pocketbook before handing me an envelope as she said, "Let me give you these before I forget." Without even looking inside of the envelope, or taking my eyes off of the road, I tucked the tickets in the center console and said, "Oh, thank you." It took us about an hour to get uptown, but it was all good. It gave us more time to talk and who knew what would come of more conversation. She had come through with the Yankee tickets, I wondered what other connects she may have. "Don't get used to Yankee tickets, though," she cautioned. "They're not a regular thing, but I got no problem hooking you up with my employee discount," she smiled. "Perfect. I want to get a pair of boots for me and my daughter," I said graciously. "I got you," she said. "I'll be calling you for rides, so you know we can work that out whenever." When we pulled up to her building, she handed me twenty-five dollars, and when I tried to give her the five back, she refused it. I took longer than expected and she had given me free Yankee tickets, it wouldn't have been absurd for her to expect a free ride. I had no problem only charging her twenty dollars. "Nah, Rah I know how much a cab costs from downtown, and I know that you looked out for me the other day with that price. Keep it." She flashed a smile and slid out of the passenger seat disappearing inside of her building.

When I got to Granny's, I parked, took the tickets from the center console, and walked inside. I was sitting at the table when I opened the envelope for the first time and was surprised to find three dated for a week away, each of them with a listed price of $100. I'm sure she could have easily sold these online for a nice amount. Perhaps she was trying to pay it forward and wait for her blessing to come back around to her as well. Regardless of her reason, the tickets, were definitely appreciated.

It wasn't hard for me to decide who I would take with me. At the time, my daughter Q and I were inseparable. My little cousin, Khylen, was six months older than my daughter and travelled many places with us. I didn't have a son, so he played the part for all intents and purposes. Thanks to that chance encounter, the three of us went to our only baseball game to date. I remember my Aunt Karyn showed up at Granny's house the day of the game with a pair of sneakers for Khylen with the Yankee symbol emblazoned on the side. These memories are priceless and wouldn't have been possible without the business that I was in. The boot connection never happened, and as a matter of fact, we never spoke to each other again. We had gotten off to such a good start, I thought it was a little strange for me to never hear from her. Hopefully nothing bad happened to her, her generosity, clearly hasn't been forgotten.

Having Foe as a passenger was a joy. During our many trips through the city, we always found fresh places to go, without any incident, or him causing trouble. The year was 2007, and after over five years of rolling together we were no longer passenger and driver; instead, just two dudes hanging out. I remember the two of us rolling across 14th Street in Lower Manhattan, headed west from the Eastside. The familiar purple glow from one of the buildings a block from the Westside Highway was coming into view. Three spotlights shining upwards were positioned in front, giving the landscape a majestic cinematic aura. The entire area was often abuzz with activity. The best part was me getting paid mostly to have fun.

One night in 2008, we were doing just that through Chinatown around 2 AM, when out of nowhere the lights and sirens of a police car flashed in my rear-view mirror. If there had been a cop car behind me, I would have noticed it; this was an unmarked car with detectives in it pulling me over. At the end of the stop, it's a good thing it was them instead of a regular blue and white unit. The officer ran my paperwork and came back to inform me, much to my surprise, that my license was suspended, and he was leaving me with a verbal warning. Had this been a regular patrol car pulling me over, I would have been headed to jail, and eventually picking Candy up from the Impound Lot. It's a good thing he told me my Pennsylvania driver's license was invalid because due to a glitch in the New York State computer system, they mailed me a new license when my old one expired. The law states you're not allowed to have a driver's license from two states, so when I got my Pennsylvania drivers' license, I turned in my New York driver's license. Somehow, the ball was dropped, I was able to keep a driver's license from both states. After the officer let me know; I pulled a quick switch and was good to drive again.

A few weeks later, while coming from my birthday dinner, I turned the corner on 127th Street and 3rd Avenue and ran smack into a police checkpoint. Checkpoints are designed specifically to catch people with outstanding warrants, suspended licenses, drunk drivers or whatever else they want to lock people up for. My non-driving ex-girlfriend, Annie was in the passenger seat, with Khylen and my daughter, Qianna, in the back. When I pulled up to the checkpoint, I handed him my New York license. As one of the cops walked to the car to check it on the computer, the other cop glared into my wallet and asked, "What's that other card there?" This cop had a keen eye for detail and was probably noticing the glint of my

Pennsylvania driver's license. To throw him off, I showed him my certification card from the gun range in Pennsylvania. "What card? This card?" I asked. Before he could muster a response, his partner returned with my New York license, and I was on my way. The ripple effect created by rolling around with my good friend, Foe, created yet another fortuitous circumstance. If I wasn't rolling with Foe that night, I never would have known about my license being invalid and would have gotten locked up at that checkpoint with my girl and the kids in the car. If that's not some "lucky" shit, I don't know what is.

Foe is the good luck charm. Thanks to him and his folks, my bills, including car payments, were always on time; I learned a good deal about myself and explored The Big Apple in a way that I hadn't before. I am forever grateful to him, as well as the people who I met through him.

I got frustrated in The Bronx and took things in my own hands to create something beautiful and lucrative for myself in Midtown. It started with snooping around in Money-Making Manhattan, where I found myself at Moon's barbershop, leading me to Blue and Vince. Regardless of my affiliation with the base, it was still up to me to market myself and build my own brand. I decided that first summer, the base wouldn't be my only stream of income, and I was going to go through my phone and reach out to everyone that I knew to market myself. Over the years, I was always willing, to help the next man. It was time for some of the people in my past to help me by opening up some doors.

Chapter 7:
Personal Connections

My definition of a personal connection is someone I would have known if I never started a car service. Personal connections include any business I generated apart from the cab base. When starting Roll with Rah, it was only logical I reached out to my old friends and family, my personal connections.

Based on my summer as a car service back in 1999, I knew chances were that my folks would be more than willing to throw some business my way. Realistically, if you have to hire someone for a service, why wouldn't you pay a person you know instead of just giving the bread to a stranger? Generational wealth is maintained by "keeping it in the family." It definitely helped I wasn't trying to market a service that wasn't necessary. The majority of New Yorkers don't drive, and at one point or another, they will NEED to hire a driver.

When I was thinking about restarting the car service, the second time around, I knew that I would have to reach out to some of my people on the streets. I figured they would have a better finger on the pulse and would be able to point me in the right direction, so to speak. Having regular jobs had left me out of touch. To grow the business, I knew that I needed to tap into all levels of society. That meant providing my services for both the working class and my unemployed massive. Necessity breeds resourcefulness, and unemployed people are nothing if not resourceful. Some people are unemployed because they can't find a job, while there are others that simply choose not to work for someone else and believe that they can do better when left to their own means. If we're honest with ourselves, we all know that you're not going to become wealthy in this world, by depending on "a job."

The first brother I chose to reach out to, was a dude from my old neighborhood named Fruquan a/k/a Fru. Fruquan is a guy I always had a lot of respect for. We're close in age which means he was born in the early seventies. Children from that era were birthed to parents who matured and came of age during the impactful, often turbulent 1960's. Growing up during the Civil Rights Movement lit a fire in the generation before ours. Things were different. For the most part, teenagers back then were in tune with the world around them as opposed to today, when most of them only care about their likes and hashtags.

The seventies were the decade when it became fashionable for some Black parents to name their children anything sounding remotely African or ancestral, in an attempt to further identify with their heritage. While it was fashionable for some, many parents took the choosing of their child's name, very seriously. These parents understood the importance of history and significance of a child's name. They taught of a past far greater than the one being taught in school; lessons revolved around lineage and the importance of honoring their ancestors. We learned that there is royalty and perseverance imprinted in our DNA. In the traditional African community, the naming of a child is key to his lot in life. It is believed that the child will take on several attributes of the name which they carry. For example, my name is Raheim. Raheim is one of the names of Allah, and it means "Most Merciful." The hope is that by naming a child with this, he will grow to be merciful and compassionate towards others.

Even though we grew up in the same development, Fru and I had different sets of friends. Growing into adulthood, we chopped it up, more often. Over time I came to know him as a man of character and integrity. A real stand-up type of dude. He was seldomly caught hanging on a corner or in front of the building, as many were known to do. I thought so highly of Fru, that back in the 90's , I got him a job working at a Patent law firm in Midtown where I had been connected to since high school. As a matter of fact, a couple of my lawyer friends from the firm advised me on parts of this project. Shout out to Florek and Endres. If you need a great Patent and Trademark attorney, hit them up. Tell them that Rah sent you. There is no way I would vouch for a person I didn't believe in.

When I told him I was thinking about getting back in the business, he exclaimed, "Do it! That's what I have been doing…well, one of the things, anyway." It was Fruquan that told me to get a black truck. At the time I was thinking blue because that was the color of my old Expedition "Tigger" that I made a lot of cash with back in the day. He told me a black suburban would be better because it would open me up for more work, like proms or businessmen. He explained that from time to time, he got work driving different musical artists around through his industry connections. Fruquan was also a part-time aspiring rapper. All of his advice was fruitful, so in my mind, I figured once I got my truck everything would be smooth sailing.

After I linked up with Candy and shouted Fru out, he told me he would pass the word along to his connects. It wasn't until the middle of August, when I finally got a call from him about his boy having a job for me. "Yo Rah…I got something for you," he excitedly clamored on the other end. "Oh yeah?" I smiled, "What's that?" "My boy has a job for you, I'm gonna give you his number so you can hit him up," he answered. I could tell he was excited for me. I was excited too; I knew it was a chance to make some real paper. "So, what's the number?" I asked. "As a matter of fact, just meet up with me and I will take you over to meet him in person." He continued, "I think it's better to meet people face to face when starting something new." The feeling was mutual. Hearing him say that reassured me, that the strong character I had always knew him to have, was indeed still intact. Some people change over the years, but Fru was still as on-point as ever.

Rob lived in Harlem, and when we met, he explained exactly what he did. It was pretty much like Fruquan had said. Rob said he was connected to the music industry, and when an artist needed a ride to a performance, the studio or airport, they called him. He had four SUVs he owned and rented to drivers, but he was always looking for more Wheelmen so that he could lower his overhead by getting rid of a vehicle or two. Everything sounded good to me. We left with the understanding that I would be there for him.

Later that night, Rob called me. I answered, "Hey Rob." "Hey Rah…Listen, I need you to pick up an artist named Joe Budden." "Okay, I'm listening," I replied. "The job pays $150, he's in Jersey City, and the show is in Queens. Are you interested?" One hundred fifty dollars was certainly nothing to write home about. I felt like I was being low balled. It would have been a bad look to turn the job down. I figured by taking this one, it would grant access to other higher paying gigs. "Yeah, I can do it. When and where?" I asked. "This Friday, I'll call you back with the details. Thanks, Rah. Have a good night." "No problem, bro" I replied.

At the time, I had never heard of Joe, so I asked around the streets to see if anyone else had. I found out Joe was considered by many, to be a rapper on the rise. At the time, 50 Cent was the hottest new thing on the streets and the word that I got was Joe was in the pipeline on the way to stardom, right behind him.

When the day came, I showed up at Joes' condominium complex early. About fifteen minutes passed before him and a couple members of his entourage made their way into my truck. Another group of his friends followed in a smaller SUV. Our journey from Jersey to Queens took less than forty minutes, with the only voices heard coming from the radio. Perhaps the others were being quiet so that Joey could get his game face on? I found the location with little trouble, and double parked with my hazard lights flashing as they filed out of Candy. The car wasn't in park but for five-seconds before they were jumping out as if they were running late or something. I drove around the corner to find a parking spot and dozed off for a quick nap. I didn't have any specific instructions for what I was supposed to do once they were in the venue, no one told me to park out front, and I figured that they would be a while. I figured wrong.

My slumber was disturbed by the blaring ring of my phone. I looked at the display, and it was Rob. I answered right away, and as soon as he realized I was on the line, he blurted out, "Hey Rah! Where are you?" Now alert, I answered, "I'm right around the corner, I will be right there." When I pulled onto the block, the other vehicle with the rest of the entourage pulled up alongside me as if they had been looking for me. I pulled up to the curb where Joe and his boys were standing, and they hurried into Candy. A few minutes after pulling off I asked, "What happened? Why'd y'all leave so quick?" "I was just going to perform," Joe responded. "I wasn't there to party." Perhaps that was the norm, but it was my first time, so I had no idea what to expect. The rest of the ride was quiet and after dropping them off back in Jersey, I called Rob to tell him I was done with the assignment, "Yo Rob, I just dropped them off." "Great...Let's meet at my place tomorrow so I can give you your money," he replied. "How's seven?" "Seven is cool. I'll see you then," I responded as we both hung up with a synchronized "Bye."

When I arrived the next day Rob explained because they couldn't find me, they wanted a discount, and I would be getting paid less than what we previously agreed upon. I didn't have a rebuttal or much leverage, even though I was never asked to stay in front of the spot. I didn't stress it because it was supposed to be the beginning of many jobs with Rob.

The next day, as I drove down the Grand Concourse, I was on the phone with my younger sister, Lashawn, telling her about the night before. She interrupted me immediately by yelling, "Oh, Joey! That's my cousin!" I chuckled. "Stop lying," I said. She laughed, "No Rah, seriously. He's, my cousin." Lashawn went on to speak to the fact "Joey lives in Jersey. He's my Aunt's son." She didn't have to go on anymore, I was convinced. I simply shook my head in amazement continuing my drive. It's crazy how small the world is.

Fast forward to Christmas Eve of 2011, when Lashawn hosted a party for her family and friends. I brought my daughter and my girlfriend at the time Annie, with me; low and behold, also attending as a guest was Lashawn's Cousin, Joey. By this point, Joey had attained much more notoriety and success. He and his girlfriend had even appeared on the reality show "Love and Hip-Hop." We chatted a bit back and forth, and I mentioned his relationship with the NBA point guard, Brandon Jennings. I picked that bit of information up somewhere while surfing the internet. He is a Knicks fan, and I am a Sixers fan so naturally we had to get in a bit of good-natured banter about our teams. I was not about to embarrass myself and act like a fan. It probably would have been inappropriate to plug the fact that I knew of a few dudes that could rap; Sco and Desperado aka Fatboy, in an attempt to get them signed. I have seen Joe a few times since then. We were at Lashawn's wedding in the Dominican Republic in 2013. He's had some of my famous jerk chicken at the summer BBQ's by the pool at my sisters' home in Jersey. To this day, I never mentioned to Joe I was the driver who picked him up that time. At this point, he's been so many places over the years, I doubt he'd remember that night.

The next time I heard from Rob, he was trying to hire me to pick up the rapper, Fabolous , from La Guardia Airport. I was definitely a fan of Fab, as he was commonly referred to, so naturally I was excited by the time we hung up. I went around the corner from my house on Morris Avenue to tell my homeboy, Gene, and smoke a blunt before I bounced to the airport. While chilling with Gene, I even wrote up a sign with the name "Fabolous" so they would know I was there to pick them up. In my giddiness, I didn't factor in that it was nearing rush hour and traffic is guaranteed to be terrible ninety percent of the time. I scooted out of The Bronx with little delay and across the Tri-boro Bridge towards the airport in Queens. As soon as I reached the Queens side of the bridge, I hit a wall of bumper-to-bumper traffic. Candy and I crept along at a snail's pace, packed in the sea of cars creeping. The weed in my system was already making me paranoid. The honking, stop and go bullshit and exhaust fumes was starting to piss me off. I was well behind schedule for the pickup when I missed my exit and had to circle around to get to the airport. As I was pulling up, I called the other truck I was supposed to linking up with. He interrupted me with, "I already picked them up." I was confused. I knew they requested two trucks, so I asked, "What about the rest of them?" "I have everyone in my truck," the driver responded. "Okay, cool," I responded. The other driver hung up. That must have been a pretty crowded ride, I thought. If they had requested two trucks, there must have been enough people to fill up two trucks, and I wasn't there when I was supposed to be. I called Rob in an attempt to explain what had happened. His words were," It's okay Rah, I get it. Things happen sometimes," but his actions showed otherwise.

That was the last time Rob gave me a call. I guess between the two incidents combined, my mistakes were too costly for his reputation or his pockets. After all, this was his business, and he made a business decision to protect his company. I completely understood. I was disappointed in myself. I saw the full potential of the opportunity I had just fucked up in two trips. I had to take accountability for blowing my chance. It hurt knowing that I had no one to blame but myself. It was a learning experience though. After dealing with Rob, I swore to always be early and confirm all of the details, beforehand. Like Rob said, "Things happen sometimes." Fortunately, every day was a new day, and a new chance to succeed. Putting my best foot forward, I decided to reach out to an old college friend of mine.

I attended Howard University, the powerhouse HBCU in Washington, DC. One of my good friends from my H.U. days, was a guy named Faoulu Mtume. His father, James Mtume, who has since passed, may he forever rest in power, was the lead artist in a group named "MTUME". He's the man the responsible for the 80s classic, "Juicy Fruit." I assumed growing up in that household meant music was the family business. Fa had an older brother, Damu, who as of summer 2002, was the President of Urban Music at Warner Brothers Records. Their two most popular artists were Jaheim and a crooner from Philly, by the name of Bilal. Both were relatively newer artists, with their debut albums released in 2001. Jaheim was the more popular artist. When Fa learned I was driving for a living, he said, "Rah, I'm sure we can throw some business your way."

Bilal preferred to use live bands for his recording sessions. At this point in time, most artists embraced the digital age and were simply using beats loaded into a computer program. The band he used was also based in Philadelphia, and Fa needed someone to drive down to pick them up and drop them back off after the sessions. There were sessions lined up for four consecutive days, which meant a lot of back-and-forth driving. Fa and I agreed upon a price of $300 a day, for a grand total of $1,200 at the end of the week. That nice lump sum I had coming to me at the end helped me ignore the amount of time I would be spending behind the wheel.

The morning I was scheduled to pick them up for the first time, I made way down the New Jersey Turnpike from New York to Philadelphia and arrived early, as I had sworn to myself I would. Their house was located on a tree-lined street, in what appeared to be a nice middle-class neighborhood. Roughly ten minutes passed before the three band members came outside, their age ranging from approximately twenty to twenty-four. I expected a much older group. From my understanding, music is a craft which takes years to master and since they were recording for a major recording artist, I thought they would be older.

The two-and-a-half-hour drive from Philly to the recording studio in Manhattan took place in near silence. I didn't know them, so I followed suit and let the radio be the only noise made in the vehicle. We got to New York around 11 AM and were met by my boy, Fa, who was in front of the recording studio in Midtown Manhattan. Fa told me that they wouldn't be done recording until about 6 PM, so I went back uptown and waited until I had to come back to get them. As it turns out, they were done closer to 5 PM.

After a quick stop at the McDonalds on 34th Street and Tenth Avenue, we were on the road heading back to Philadelphia. The ride back down was way different from the ride up. On this trip, they got back in the truck full of life. It had been an early morning pick up. I'm sure it contributed to the somberness that morning. Regardless, on the ride back down, we jabbered like a couple of old friends to the point they offered to house me overnight. That was indeed a blessing for me. Although, had I been forced to drive back to New York and then be back in Philadelphia the next morning, I would have no complaints. However, the invitation to stay not only saved a lot of time, but it also saved about $100 worth of gas. I parked, and as we made our way into the house, the first thing I noticed is they didn't lock the door when they left that morning. It seemed strange but maybe someone else was upstairs? I walked upstairs to discover the place was basically a flop house, and they didn't lock the door because there was nothing of value to steal. There was an old television in the corner fixed on MTV which they used to consume all genres of music. I was surprised that they weren't limiting themselves to only rap or soul videos. They appreciated all artists. This crew was truly what some folks would call grunge musicians. I spent about three days with them and never saw any of them take a shower. We spent most of our time watching MTV and smoking weed.

At the end of the fourth day, while driving back to Philly for what was supposed to be my final time, the boys and I were just talking about what their plans were for the rest of the weekend. It was Saturday, so who knew what they had going after I dropped them off. They told me that they would be playing in a festival over the weekend. It sounded like something worth sticking around for, so I decided to stay another night, just not with them. However, I did offer transportation for them to get to the gig.

I strolled around downtown Philadelphia that evening, looking for something to wear. I had been back and forth driving for four days, with no shower or change of clothes. I wasn't about to spend another day, especially on the weekend in the same things I had worn all week. I kept it simple and bought a football jersey. The jersey was a St. Louis Rams Marshall Faulk replica. He wasn't playing anymore, so most people buying throwbacks spent a lot more than the $30 I spent. A young dude in his late teens chuckled, "If you aren't going to buy the official jersey, what's the point?" The point was the $70 I was saving by buying a replica. I needed something functional, I wasn't looking to make a fashion statement; nor did I bother to explain that to him. I found a hotel nearby, checked-in, and immediately went upstairs to my room for a much-needed shower and shave before settling in for a good night's rest.

The next day, I left the hotel, to pick the boys up to take them to the park where the festival was taking place. I thought I would have an issue finding parking, and much to my surprise, there wasn't the slightest problem. After a quick unloading, we walked across the jam-packed festival grounds amongst people of all ages, making their rounds visiting various vendors' booths. There was still about ninety minutes before the boys were scheduled to perform so while they were backstage getting ready, I meandered around the crowd, taking in the scene and eye candy of Philadelphia. Before I knew it, so much time had elapsed, the ninety minutes was down to nine and the boys appeared on the stage for a last check of their gear before they began playing back up to the legendary singer, Karen Clark. The half-hour set concluded with an ovation complete with whistles and airhorns and judging by the crowd's reaction, I could tell they we were equally enthralled with her performance. To this day, it is a memory emblazoned in my mind for which I thank God I was blessed enough to experience. After the boys broke down their gear, we began the trek back across the festival grounds in the direction of Candy. "Where are you guys headed from here?" I asked. "We have to play at church," one of them responded. "The grind never stops." "Don't I know it," I chuckled. I was enjoying myself so much, it was almost as if I didn't want to go home. "I can take y'all to that. It's no big deal. It makes sense I get a little church in me before I head back." "Bet. Good looks," another responded. "That'll save so much trouble." It was a short drive over to the boys' church for the performance and after they were done, the time had finally come for me to say my goodbyes and head back to New York. It wasn't a goodbye as much as it was a simple "Later…" The boys were always in New York recording and promised to look me up the next time they were around. Eventually, they did exactly that a few months later but I was too busy chasing that money on a Friday night, so I didn't go to meet them in their hotel, and they never tried to reach out again. In retrospect, I should have gone to see them, when they came back to town. There are more important things than money.

The Tuesday after getting back from Philadelphia, I met up with Fa in the city to pick up my check. I told him how much I appreciated the job, in addition to the great time I had chilling with the band. Fa told me the feeling was mutual, and I would be hearing from him the next time they needed a ride. As it turned out, the next time was an airport trip for Bilal; he was headed out on tour with his real band, not the boys he used for the studio session. I knew transporting this many people meant I would need a second vehicle, so without hesitation, I gave my boy, Fruquan, a call to plug him in. This was the first of many jobs I worked with Fa over the next year. Whenever the need arose, be it an artist or someone in the office, I was the first that Fa would call. I appreciate the love and support. Thanks a lot Ulu.

In the fall of 2003, by happenstance or fate, another personal connection fueled a large part of my business. Mike was a younger guy I knew from my old neighborhood; his older brother, Reg, and I used to hang out in my early twenties. He was about seven years younger than me, and one day when I was driving down Lexington Avenue, I saw Mike walking down the street. I beeped my horn to get his attention, and he motioned for me to pull over. He climbed into Candy, and I pulled off with us listening to the radio, talking about the new Jay Z and Beyonce song. The song ended, and almost on cue Mike and I got to talking about my new business venture. "You know...I know a guy that's been taking trips out of town on the regular, making bank," he commented. "K.K. from

Metro North…you know who I'm talking about?" When he first said the name, it didn't ring any bells for me. Additionally, this kid had gone to school with Mike, and that meant that he was much younger than me. Typically, unless someone was a young kid that I knew from seeing on my block, I didn't know them by name. However, the way neighborhoods were set up, chances are if he was from my old hood, then I had seen him around at least one time or another. "Bro he's making so much bread moving coke," Mike continued. "He's back and forth to PA."

Up until this point, I had only made some local drug runs around New York City, the furthest being upstate with Dap, but never out of state. Dap was only selling weed; interstate cocaine distribution carried a much stiffer penalty. God forbid, someone moving coke across state lines was ever caught. The law permits each state passed through the right to fully prosecute for the possession and transportation of drugs, even though you were never caught in that state. Obviously, it's supposed to be a deterrent against transporting; but what isn't considered is the desperation one feels to sell drugs out of town or, in my case, transport people selling drugs out of town. High risks equal high rewards, and at that point, the person has already decided to act out of survival. I already made my mind up that I was all-in and had long since kicked all fear to the curb.

In the places like New York City where illegal narcotics have been a problem for years, those police forces have had billions of dollars thrown at them to develop all types of surveillance and anti-drug task forces. In most of the rural American neighborhoods, law enforcement was typically behind the curve, making it easier for someone out of town to mosey in, and supply the locals. Most small towns just weren't prepared to deal with a sudden influx of illegal drugs, and if said supplier is smart, he's usually long gone or on his way out of town by the time the cops realize what's going on. Additionally, fiends in small towns have a harder time getting access to certain drugs because there are usually less people participating in the drug trade. In order for the town to have access, someone has to bring them in. This means a seller can charge much more in a small town than he would in the city. Prices are often doubled and depending on the drug, as much as quadrupled.

I was fully aware of the potential risks and rewards when I finally answered Mike and told him, "I'm down. Holler at him and set something up for me." That's all Mike needed to hear, and about a week later, K.K. hit me up. "Yo Rah, what's good? It's K.K. Yo can you come grab me from the park?" It wasn't just any park, it was a "work out park"; a park with strength building equipment like chin up and dip bars. I pulled up to the park to find K.K. finishing up a set of pull ups. I rolled down the passenger window and shouted, "Yo K.K.!" He walked over to the car, got in and we were off. "Getting your workout on, I see. I need to get back on my shit," I said . "Yeah, I just came home not too long ago…you know how that goes. I got so used to working out inside, I'm just trying to keep the routine up." "I feel that" I said in agreement. K.K. was smart.

On the ride to his building, I recognized why he called me to pick him up from the park. For starters, the park was pretty far away from his crib, and he had to get home. Second, he needed to meet up with me to feel me out and see if he was comfortable with me carrying out his mission. Additionally, riding in my car gave him an opportunity to identify it if he ever needed to. After deciding I was the right man for the job, K.K. mentioned it wouldn't be him making the trip down to Pennsylvania. He was sending one of his people, which made perfect sense. After all, he was still on probation and couldn't risk getting caught out of town, much less having drugs in his possession. "Tomorrow night," K.K. interrupted my train of thought, "You gotta pick up my guy, Heavy. I'll call you again, but you gotta meet him on 102nd Street and First Ave. How much are you charging me?" "I got you. The whole run is gonna cost you $300," I replied. Three hundred dollars was the same price I charged the musicians. Knowing the risks involved, I should've charged him way more. "That's cool," he responded calmly. The money I was charging him wasn't even a drop in the bucket compared to what he was probably pulling in. "Tomorrow night," he said, dapping me as he got out of the car.

On the next day, I showed up to meet Heavy on the corner of 102nd Street and First Avenue, just as I had agreed. I was waiting for about thirty minutes before a heavy-set Spanish dude in his mid-to-late twenties finally sauntered up to my truck with a small duffle bag. "You Rah?" he asked. I nodded to signal he had the right car. "Yeah...hop in..." I said coolly. He climbed up into Candy, and we were off towards the George Washington Bridge to make our way towards Pennsylvania. I didn't have a GPS to navigate us, so I said to Heavy, "I hope you know where we're going." He flashed a smile, "Don't worry. I've taken this trip mad times. I got you."

As we rode, we chatted to pass the time. It took us about two hours, to reach our exit on the highway. We exited the PA Turnpike and were on the local road that was supposed to be a straight shot to our destination. About five minutes down the road, we both caught a glimpse of a police car parked diagonally, facing towards oncoming traffic. I'm sure in small towns, speed traps were a common thing, so that sight alone didn't raise any alarms. We continued the drive for about another half a mile down the road when I saw the state troopers were in the process of setting up a DUI checkpoint. The site hadn't been fully activated yet; they were unloading the canines from their units as I pulled up.

As I slowed to a stop, an officer who appeared to be in his early 60's, approached the driver's window and said, "Good evening. This is a DUI checkpoint. Have you been drinking this evening?" I looked him square in the eye. Surely, they were doing more than simply asking if people were drinking at DUI checkpoints. Either way my answer wasn't going to change. "I don't drink, I'm a Muslim," I responded bluntly. It wasn't a lie. I didn't begin to study the religion of Islam until 2004 when my father died, and I was going through a sober period in my life. I hadn't been drinking for months. The officer didn't even bother with a verbal response and waved us through without a second thought.

We arrived at our destination after another five-mile drive down the same road. When we arrived, there was a Puerto Rican kid from Spanish Harlem waiting for us. Apparently, he had been down there since the last time drop off. Heavy and the kid dapped each other up and began to chatter. "Son, you won't believe what just happened to us," Heavy chirped. "We dead ass just ran into a DUI check." "Word? Y'all lucky for real…" responded the other kid. "Be happy they didn't search the vehicle!" he laughed. That's when I found out there was one hundred grams of cocaine in t duffle bag. One hundred grams of coke retailed for $2,500 at the time, and with the out-of-town mark up, could see a value of upwards of $10,000 easily. "Shit, there's nothing linking the drugs in that bag to me," Heavy said as he slyly chuckled. I understood that to mean, had we gotten searched, he had no intention of speaking up to take ownership of the drugs. I knew what Heavy was implying. The law states, unless a passenger speaks up to say otherwise, the contents found in a vehicle belong to the driver. "Yo Rah, I'm staying down here," Heavy told me. "Don't even trip, just go back the way you came, it's a straight shot." "I got you," I said, partially relieved I was driving back by myself. In my opinion, Heavy was untrustworthy. "Be safe."

I walked back to Candy, started the engine, and backed out of the driveway to make my way back to New York. On my way back, I ran into the DUI checkpoint again, now in full swing. As I eased to a complete stop, I was greeted by three officers, one of whom twisted his neck in all sorts of unnatural ways to see inside the vehicle and sniff for weed or alcohol. At the same time, another officer made his way around to the passenger window to peek in the backseat, and ultimately hand me some literature warning against the hazards or driving while intoxicated. The whole ordeal was so amusing I was laughing out loud. We didn't receive a fraction of the attention on our way in, and we had a duffle bag full of cocaine. Here I was on my way out, job well-done, and garnering the attention of all three cops at the checkpoint. I definitely used one of my nine lives and got away with some illegal shit at that DUI checkpoint.

In total, I did two more runs with K.K. and his boys. I couldn't get past the idea that Heavy would've thrown me under the bus had we been caught that day. There is no honor in these streets anymore.

In 2007, I got the chance to do a cool job with one of my Pennsylvanian neighbors. Rollwithrah had been in business for just under five years, when my neighbor, Mark, who drove a fifteen-passenger van, was approached about a family that would be traveling to New York City. In total, there would be about seventeen people who needed ground transportation while in town. Mark normally used his van to shuttle commuters back and forth between The Pocono Mountains and New York City. The cost of living in New York was a determining factor in many people choosing to migrate to the much more affordable Poconos. Unfortunately, the job market didn't follow them to the mountains, and many of them were forced to still work their old jobs in the city. Even still, people saved a lot of money by living in PA and commuting to NYC.

When we spoke, Mark filled me in on the details about the family coming to town. They would be arriving at Newark Airport in New Jersey on a flight from South Carolina, Friday afternoon. After being picked up from the airport, they needed to be taken to their hotel in New York near JFK Airport. The family reunion they were coming to town for was taking place on that Saturday, and they wanted us to scoop them from the hotel and take them to the hall in Queens. After the reunion was over, we were to bring them back to their hotel and then return to get them on Sunday for their departure flight from Newark. The banquet hall was in the same borough as the hotel, so I knew I wouldn't be doing too much driving. The gig became that much sweeter when Mark told me I would be making $400.

When Friday came, we arrived at the airport to pick up the group as planned. It was a mixed party of men, women, and children with multiple generations present. The youngest of the group were little children around the age of five and the oldest being the Grandfather who appeared to be in his late 60's. The entire group had deep country accents, and as we were figuring out which vehicle would hold whom, one of the heavy-set sisters in her mid-to-late thirties, hopped in the front seat of my truck and said, "Y'all can stand around deciding if ya wanna, but I am sitting right here." Sensing the frustration was growing, one of her brothers pleaded with the group, "Everybody just get in either vehicle, so we could get on out of here and on to the hotel."

As we were leaving New Jersey, I figured it made the most sense to take the Holland Tunnel to cut through Lower Manhattan to get to Queens instead of taking the George Washington Bridge. The bridge route was probably packed given the time of day, and although NYC traffic is a part of the luster, I try to avoid it at all costs. It was their first time in New York, and I wanted them to see as much as they could, even if the only opportunity was on the ride to the hotel. "Yeah, this is New York," I said, "the city that never sleeps, as they say. There are just so many people you never know who you will see walking down the street." At that exact moment and almost on cue, as I looked to my right out of the passenger window, I saw Steve Harvey walking down the sidewalk, donning a wide brimmed hat and puffing a cigar. "See, there goes Steve Harvey right there," I blurted out. The sister in the front seat quickly turned to verify what I had just said and yelled out, in a southern drawl, "There he is. There goes Steve!"

It took us about an hour to get to the hotel with all the traffic. I imagined it must have felt like twenty minutes for them. They never stopped marveling at attractions, pointing and talking the entire time. New York can be overwhelming at times, especially for first-time visitors. As we pulled up to the hotel, we quickly unloaded and confirmed the pickup time for the following days' events.

When Saturday arrived, we picked them up from the hotel as we had planned. Mark and I spent the better portion of that day parked around the corner from where the reunion was taking place. The hardest part of this particular job was the waiting time. The reunion finally ended, and the family filed out of the hall into a large group in front of the building. The group decided amongst themselves, the men would ride back with me, and the women and children would go with Mark. While enroute back to their hotel, I overheard one of the brothers say to the others, "Man I'm sad we ain't gonna get a chance to see the real New York City. I want to see Harlem, The Bronx…all that stuff." I empathized with him. All they had gotten to experience was the quick trip through Chinatown and the brief ride from the hotel in Queens to the church in Queens. As a native New Yorker, I knew that wasn't even the tip of the iceberg. We hadn't done much driving around, and they did agree to pay me well for my services, so I decided to extend a courtesy on behalf of RollwithRah.

As we pulled into the hotel parking lot, I put Candy in park and asked, "So do you guys want me to come back and get you for a tour of the city?" One of the brother's raised an eyebrow and asked, "How much are you going to charge us?"

I laughed. "There will be no charge. Y'all cool…I can take you on a quick spin through the city free of charge. It's no problem." They were Black like me and from the South, just like my family originally was. We are all related somewhere down the line so, why not look out for them? I would have wanted someone to do the same for me if I were in their position. "I'll be back for y'all around a little later. Get some rest," I said as they climbed out of Candy and closed the doors. "Thank you," said the brother.

When I came back to the hotel that night to get them, they were already downstairs waiting and ready for their joy ride. The oldest brother climbed in the front seat, with their Father in the second row, and the other brothers next to and behind him in the third rows respectively. We pulled out the hotel and headed straight for The Bronx. Two of the brothers asked if I knew where they could get some weed. I chuckled, "For sure, I got you." They had no idea how well connected I was. The Father, who hadn't said much the entire time finally parted his mouth to say in the heaviest southern accent of them all, "Just stop by a liquor store so I can get me a small bottle of Hennessy and I'll be fine." It began to feel like a normal hold call with some of my regular passengers in the hood. We grabbed the bud from my boy TL in The Bronx and stopped at a liquor store around the corner.

The joy ride was in full effect, and before we left The Bronx, I made sure to drive them by Yankee Stadium. After passing by the Stadium, we headed across the Macomb's Dam Bridge into the heart of Harlem. It would have been a shame for them to go home after visiting New York and not seeing Harlem. I drove them by the Holcombe Rucker basketball courts on 155th Street and 8th Avenue. Ever since the 50's, the Rucker has showcased a variety of NBA legends on its concrete courts. It's a rite of passage for all great NBA ball players, from Kareem Abdul Jabbar and Julius Erving to the late Kobe Bryant. Even modern-day legends such as Kevin Durant and LeBron James have had their moment to shine at The Rucker. Even Dick Vitale, the famed basketball announcer, called a game at the Rucker, which I was in attendance for. The court grounds are truly sacred. The second stop after Rucker Park, was 125th street, home of the world-famous Apollo Theatre. Rocking The Apollo was pivotal in helping launch the careers of legendary artists such as Ella Fitzgerald, Billie Holiday, James Brown, Diana Ross & The Supremes, Gladys Knight & the Pips, The Jackson 5, Patti LaBelle, Marvin Gaye, Luther Vandross, Stevie Wonder, just to name a few. The Apollo Theatre is a staple in Black culture and a must see for anyone visiting Harlem.

We left 125th Street and took a quick drive ten blocks drive north to what is known as Strivers' Row. Strivers' Row is a collection of brownstone houses in western Harlem, each of which is a designated landmark. You would never know there were multi-million-dollar properties sitting right in the middle of the hood, unless some told you or you were from there. From Strivers' Row, it was a quick five-minute drive to the Westside Highway entrance on 125th Street. We were headed downtown for the final leg of their New York City tour. No tour of New York City is complete without them seeing the man-made marvel that is 42nd Street. For this part of the tour, the inner child leapt out of my passengers. As we crossed 46th Street, one of the brothers pointed out of the window grinning from ear to ear, "Aye look at that giant M&M!" The rest of the passengers looked skywards at the forty-foot-tall M&M candy, hanging on the side of the M&M store. All their eyes twinkled with delight like a little kid's at Disney World. Even as a native New Yorker, I sometimes found myself still getting excited driving amongst the bright lights and sounds of Times Square.

By the time we got back to the hotel, it was nearing 4 AM and I was slated to be back to take them to the airport in four hours. "Aye Bruh, it's almost four in the morning. I have a spare bed in my room, you can crash for a few hours instead of having to go home and then come back." "Aww man. I appreciate that, seriously," I graciously replied. "No problem, Bruh. You took care of us; it's only right we return the favor to make it easy on you. You don't need to be driving tired."

The next morning, we woke up and got everyone packed up. I was already sitting in front of the hotel waiting for Mark when he arrived. "How did you get here so fast?" he asked. "I ended up staying with them, actually," I responded with a smile. Mark let out a chuckle, "You really do have a way with people, boy I swear." "That's my gift Bro, I can't help it," I laughed back. When we arrived at the airport, before we parted ways, the oldest brother walked up and said, "Thanks for everything Rah. We had a blast…If there is ever anything that you need, just get word down to us and we will be sure to get it up here to you." I sincerely appreciated the offer and gesture. At one point, I sent out the word through Mark to try and get in touch with them, but the attempt was unsuccessful. if any of you brothers are reading this book, or even the sister for that matter, reach out to me.

Mark was able to hook me up with a few other jobs after that family. Driving a shuttle meant he was always meeting new commuters, one of whom was a woman named Patricia. Patricia, like so many of us, the move to the mountains due in part to the high cost of living in the New York City area. Patty was married to a guy, ironically enough, named Patrick. When we met, they had two kids under five--a little boy and a little girl. Once they moved to The Poconos, Patty's parents missed their only daughter and grandkids terribly. Patty 's father was named Mangol. Mangol and his wife were originally from the South American country, Guyana. The way they described water from the Caribbean Sea and the Atlantic Ocean washing upon its shores, I imagined it a beautiful place to visit. When I would come to pick up Mangol for his trips, he was almost always traveling alone, even though he was still married. There's only one time the Grandmother travelled either with Mangol or the rest of the family. I don't know what that was about.

When Patty and Patrick moved to The Poconos, Mangol was miserable in New York City without them. It didn't take long before he and his wife bought a house on the same block as their daughter. The closest airport is in Allentown, and about a fifty-minute drive from our part of The Poconos. The majority of outbound flights typically forced people to have to catch a connecting flight to another plane somewhere to get you to your destination; the majority of people living in The Poconos still flew out of the New York Metro area when traveling. This is where my services came into play.

One day Mark called and explained he had some passengers that needed to get to Newark Airport, from The Poconos, and they wanted to know how much I would charge to take them. Fortunately for them, they only lived about fifteen minutes from my house in The Poconos. I still worked in New York, so more than likely, I would need to drive up anyway, so essentially this family was about to pay me to go where I was already going. "A hundred fifty bucks," is what I told Mark on the phone. The airport was over a hundred miles away from where they lived. Any cab from The Poconos would have easily charged them a minimum of $200. At the time, a tank of gas cost me about $70 or $80; so, at worst, even if my gas tank was on empty, I still stood to make a $40 to $50 profit. I also didn't want to charge them too much; I wasn't going too far out of my way at all.

When I pulled up to get them for that first trip together, I wasn't sure cutting them a break on the price was a good choice. The pickup was Mangol, Patty, Pat and the kids. Mangol sat up front with me wearing a stern and disgruntled expression. I assumed he was pissed his wife wasn't coming along. Despite being in his mid-seventies, he looked good for his age and gave the appearance and presence of a man a decade younger. Mangol sat in the front seat with his expression unwavering as we began our journey towards the highway. People are often guarded until they get to know the person a little better, and this was especially true with a gentleman of Mangol's age. Once I broke through the gruff exterior, it was clear I had made the right decision by giving them a discount. I had some Stevie Wonder and some Bob Marley CDs loaded in the disc changer to play for as an icebreaker on our drive along 80 East to Newark. The music that I play is usually catered to my clientele, so it made sense someone from The Caribbean would appreciate some Bob Marley. As expected, Bob eased the mood of the vehicle. The music was a vessel for us to get to know each other. Eventually, I would be welcomed in both Mangol's and Pat's homes. In fact, we got so close, Foe even joined me for a beer in Mangols' house one day.

About a year or so after our original meeting, Patty accepted a job offer which moved her family down to Orlando Florida and her husband, Patrick, got a job with one of the newer tourist resorts. The housing crash prevented Patty from selling their home in The Poconos. She and Patrick ended up renting the house out to someone with the understanding her dad, Mangol, would collect the rent money and take care of any business necessary. Of course, once they moved, Mangol longed for his family to the point he would fly down to Florida and spend most of the winter. It never failed, whenever the time came for the trip down and back Patty called to set up transportation.

At one point, Mangol hired a realtor hoping to sell his home and move to Florida. Trying to sell a house when the real estate market is down meant they were advised to drop their asking price. His wife would hear nothing of it, nor did she seem to be at all bothered by the family moving to Florida. I'm no psychologist, but my speculation was she was irritated by the amount of attention that Mangol showered on his daughter and grandchildren. Mangol and Patty were very close, and he used to always say, "There is nothing that we can't discuss between her and me." The love that he felt for his baby girl simply transferred to his grandchildren.

On Easter Sunday 2008, Mangol was flying back from Florida and needed a drop off at his house in The Poconos. Coincidentally, I was in New York working and was headed home the same day to be with my family. It may have been because of the holiday, but on this Easter Sunday, JFK was overwhelmingly swamped with travelers. Mangol's plane was terribly delayed, and at the time he didn't own a cell phone. Patty told me that he didn't check any luggage, so we figured that he would be curbside about twenty minutes after his plane was due to land. However, with such a significant delay, there was no way to know when he would be arriving. After 9/11, airports around the country changed their policies about idling waiting for passengers, so the police don't allow you to linger at the curb for too long. My Niece, Jazmin, was waiting with me and though she wasn't saying much about it, I could tell she was becoming more impatient the longer we waited.

We sat by the curb, with no sight of Mangol for about an hour before I called Patty to make sure that he hadn't missed his flight. She confirmed Mangol boarded the plane but didn't mention the delay, nor did I think to ask. This was turning into a much more of an ordeal than I had bargained for, and with Easter Sunday rapidly passing by and an impatient fifteen-year-old in the car, I needed to figure out what was going on. There was a long line of cars waiting curbside, so I circled around and parked Candy at the back of the line. "I'm going to go in here and check to see what's going on. I'll be right back, ok?" I said to Jazmine. We both knew she didn't have a say whether it was okay or not, but it was the courteous thing to do. She nodded in agreement, and I headed towards the entrance of the gate. I needed to be quick. It was a huge risk leaving an unlicensed fifteen-year-old in the car. If Port Authority pulled up and asked her to move it, she wouldn't be able to, but I needed to find Mangol. I looked at him as if he were my father in need of a ride from the airport. Kennedy Airport is about a hundred and twenty miles away from The Poconos; I shuddered at the thought of what a cab would have charged him to get home.

I was excited for the Easter dinner my mother was cooking; however, I accepted a job, and it was my responsibility to make sure my passenger got home safely. Regular cab drivers wouldn't have spent the time waiting or hunting Kennedy Airport for a passenger, but fortunately for Mangol, he was RollingwithRah. Going the extra mile for my people is just something that came with the package when you hired me. After searching the airport for roughly two hours, I eventually found Mangol waiting in the wrong location. In addition to the flight delay, he had gotten confused winding up at the wrong terminal. We made our way back to the car, both of us relieved in more ways than one. Not one officer came to try and get Jazmin to move the truck the entire time I was searching for Mangol. I eventually got us all back to The Poconos safely, without incident or ticket. As a result, two things happened because of the trouble we had finding Mangol that day. For starters, Patty never let her dad travel without a cell phone, again. Secondly, Mangol's wife gave me a twenty-dollar tip while thanking me, repeatedly. It wasn't about the money; I did what I felt was the right thing to do.

Over the years, Mangol became a bit of a mentor to me. In my eyes, this man was rich, and it had little to do with financial security. He was rich because he had the three things that mattered the most: his health, his family, and his wallet. If it's possible to attain those three things at any age, you should consider yourself blessed to have all three and as rich as Mangol. He often gave me wise words on parenting and relationships, hell even restaurant tips. I will never forget him taking me to lunch at a local eatery I had driven by over a hundred times since moving to Pennsylvania, but never stopped at. One day when I was dropping him off, he said, "Raman," (as he used to mispronounce my name) "come and get me one day boy, so we go and get a little bit to eat. It's not always just business yuh know." I am glad that I took him up on his offer.

The restaurant had a drab exterior, easily dating back to the 70's, and resembled the sort of down-trodden place locals would gather at on a Friday night. The interior, however, was a completely different story. We passed through the doors and headed onto their side deck, where unbeknownst to us, we were stepping into a party. There was a small pool outside, fully equipped with a bar and a DJ who was knee deep in a set full of up-tempo songs. There was no way of seeing any of this from the road.

The two of us sat and drank the beers we ordered with our lunch as Mangol played the role of wise old teacher, and I the humble appreciative pupil. My father had passed away in 2004, so I jumped at the chance to glean some knowledge from an older man. Mangol told me of his days back in Guyana, when he used to be a drunkard. He told me his own family would cross to the other side of the street when they saw him coming, either out of shame or embarrassment. More importantly, Mangol explained how he kicked the drinking habit and started handling his responsibilities as a man. Mangol wasn't aware of the many ways I related to his story. I had been known to enjoy the company of a nice drink, Jack Daniel's to be specific. Fortunately, like much of my other self-destructive behaviors, heavy drinking is now a thing of the past. I still enjoy a taste here and there, but thankfully, I'm not the functioning lush I once was. I even comped one of his holds on a day he needed to run some local errands. He had already paid me with his wisdom.

Two years later, Mangol was still living in The Poconos instead of dropping the asking price and moving down to the warm southern air. His wife insisted on "living her life" instead of enjoying her golden years in the mountains or down south with the family; and elected to go back and forth working and visiting her girlfriends in New York. In my opinion, she was almost seventy and should have long given up the chase for dollars and hanging out. One day, a snowstorm hit while his wife was at work. When he saw how much snow was falling, Mangol was worried his wife wouldn't be able to get in the house after being dropped off by her co-worker, so he went outside to shovel a path for her. While shoveling, Mangol suffered a heart attack, and passed away on that winter day in 2010. His last phone call was to his baby girl, Patty. He told her he had been shoveling snow, but now he felt lightheaded and short of breath. She yelled into the phone, "CALL THE AMBULANCE DADDY!!" Mangol quietly answered back, "It's too late for that. I just wanted to tell you that I love you and to tell the kids that grandpa loves them always." His wife arrived home about an hour later to find him lying on the floor in the foyer. His son-in-law, Patrick, reached out to me to deliver some of the saddest news I've ever received over the phone. Mangol touched my life by becoming a valued friend of mine, and he will forever be remembered fondly.

There was one more set of Pennsylvania passengers who came to me through Mark and the van service. Mark was connected with them similarly to the way he was with Mangol and his family. He was standing outside of the park-and-ride in The Poconos as he did most weekday mornings, when he was approached by a Black woman in her mid to late forties named Laurel. Just as Pat had done, she asked about having her and her family transported to the airport. Mark's focus was the shuttle, so all other driving jobs fell into my eternally grateful hands. Mark gave me a call one day to explain the job, and it didn't take much talking for me to quickly schedule them in. Laurel and her family lived in East Stroudsburg at the time, which wasn't anywhere near fifteen minutes from my house in The Poconos, but it was still convenient because it is in the direction I would be traveling to get to the NY/NJ area.

It wasn't too long after I pulled up to their house before the family came outside. The first one out of the door carrying a few pieces of luggage was her husband, Donnell. The first thing I noticed about Dee (as his friends call him) was how large of a man he was. Dee is big, and not as in fat or tall; as in, his muscles had muscles. As it turns out, he is a bit of a workout fanatic. At first glance, one could easily stereotype him as a big dumb jock; but after knowing Dee for the several years, he would be more accurately described as a renaissance man for several reasons. First, Donnell has been an artist since he was a child. His art was a way for him to, "get his mind off the bullshit he had to deal with in reality,". Drawing was his earliest form of expression. In addition to that, he's a chef by trade and even went as far as take his artistic expression to the kitchen, masterfully created his own culinary inventions.

His most memorable rice dish, "Blackanese" fried rice was to die for; the additional zest coming from one of the many jars of homemade sauces he kept on the bar inside of his man cave. They all had creative names like "That hot shit for greens" and "fire mango." Lastly, Dee was a musician, specializing in the guitar and had written a few songs. Unsurprisingly, we formed a genuine friendship. I had the pleasure of visiting them after they moved from East Stroudsburg to their new house in Tobyhanna. I was genuinely happy for them, and the move would prove beneficial for both of us. Tobyhanna is much closer to Blakeslee than East Stroudsburg, and that made pickups and drop-offs even more convenient. Additionally, they moved into a much larger house, one that was now equipped with a garage for Dee's stuff.

The garage wasn't the only perk of the new place in Tobyhanna. Dee transformed the multi-roomed basement into the ultimate man cave; one fully equipped with a big screen television, reclining furniture, and a theatre quality surround sound system. One of the rooms off to the side, which he aptly named "The Panic Room" was converted into a complete home gym. Inside, was everything you would ever need to get in shape. There were five different weight machines, with a rack of dumbbells lining the wall ranging in weight from 10 to 100 pounds. There was even a treadmill in the corner for when it was too cold to train outside. The walls were covered with mirrors like you would find in any commercial gym, and he went as far having a padded floor installed just in case a weight was accidentally dropped. It wasn't until after actually seeing the inside of "The Panic Room" did I know exactly how Dee maintained his physique.

Over the years, we made about three or four airport runs together. Outside of the driver-passenger relationship, we related to each other—much like my relationship with Mangol, because we thought similarly. Both Dee and I are fans of science-fiction movies and were smart enough to realize if we wanted to have a house and peace of mind without being rich, the best place for us was the beautiful Pocono Mountains. In fact, when I am home, Dee is basically the only person I leave my house to visit. Who would pass up the chance to have a meal prepared by a professional chef, after a good work out?

Who passes up food and a movie on a state-of-the-art home theatre? I don't, especially when it's at my friend's house. I treat going home to The Poconos as a mini vacation, and an evening over at Dee's house is a part of the relaxing time which has fortunately become the norm.

If not for the personal connection I had with Mark, my friendships with Donnell and Mangol would never have grown as they did. Honestly, I probably would have never met them. Mark definitely blessed me. Having those few passengers turn out to be winners, and those experiences and memories are priceless. I know I have said it a thousand times but, thank you Bro.

I would like to tell you about a guy, that I mentioned earlier when telling y'all about the Six Flags trip. Darren and I have known each other, since I was eight years old. I am over fifty now, and if I've learned anything, it's that forty plus year friendships don't grow on trees. I am pleased to say Darren is and will always be one of my closest friends. The two of us started playing little league baseball together at the age of ten. Whether we were out of town together, or just chilling in the hood, we've done it all. While I was always bouncing from one fling to another, Darren was much more conservative and was seemingly waiting for Mrs. Right. His patience paid off in the spring of 2008 when he was married to his lovely wife, Tina. Two years later, in 2010 they were blessed with the arrival of a beautiful baby girl, Jayla. It was Tina and Darren's first child. He is a year older than me, so I felt like he waited quite a while to have his first child. After his daughter was born, Darren called me to come and get them from the hospital in lower Manhattan. Baby girl was being discharged and would be coming home for the very first time, so I had no intention of charging them for the trip. After loading the three of them into Candy, we made the quick half an hour drive uptown to their apartment located along the southern tip of Harlem, just north of Central Park.

I slowed Candy to a stop directly in front of the building and shifted her into park. Tina opened her handbag and began reaching inside, "How much Rah?" I smiled. "There's no charge Tina. You know I would do anything for my boy, Darren." "Don't be silly Rah. This is your livelihood, and I wouldn't want my baby girl being driven home in anyone else's vehicle, but yours. I wouldn't trust them." That really meant a lot to me. "Thank you, Rah" she said warmly while sliding a $20 bill in my hand. They gathered their things out of Candy and made their way to the building.

A few years afterwards, Tina was diagnosed with Cancer. She continued to be a great wife and parent up until the year 2020, when she passed away due to complications after contracting Covid-19. Covid-19 was a plague that changed the trajectory of life for the entire world, claiming millions of lives across the globe.

It was easy to get the support of the people I knew, because RollwithRah provided a basic necessity. Again, if you must give the money to someone, why not make it one of your own? I assume, that was my Mother's thinking in 2006.

On the low corner of Candy's windshield, I still have a PBA sticker from the year 2006. PBA is an abbreviation for the Police Benevolent Association, a labor organization representing the interests of police officers. If an officer is killed in the line of duty, then they typically assume the responsibility of helping provide for the slain officer's family. Police departments are huge families or gangs; however you want to look at it and like any successful group, they take care of their own. Needless to say, a support sticker on the windshield could go a long way.

Like many people, my Mother always loved to visit midtown Manhattan to see Broadway shows. On this occasion, she was headed to see a play with one of her friend's, Marie. Marie lived in Co-op City in The Bronx, so it made more sense for the two of them meet up at my Grandmother's house in Harlem. My mother typically drove her own vehicle, but parking around the Theatre District is limited, so driving to the show wasn't an option. My mother asked me, "How much would you charge to take us to the show, come back to get us afterwards, and then drop Marie off at her apartment in The Bronx?" "Don't be silly Ma, I am not going to charge you," I replied as any son would. "No, I know this is your business, I will pay you." After a brief silence, I finally answered, "Okay. I'll charge you the rate for one hour. That's thirty-five bucks." "Okay! I'll see you later baby." I felt weird charging my Mom, but I also knew she wasn't going to budge on me not charging her.

It was a brisk day in the middle of winter. The sun was shining brightly when Marie shuffled up to Granny's place sometime in the mid-afternoon. Shortly after, we piled into Candy to start our journey downtown. I was wearing a large, puffy, down coat—the type of coat that made wearing a seatbelt uncomfortable, so I decided not to wear one as we drove down Fifth Avenue. As we neared Marcus Garvey Park, we pulled up to the stop sign on the corner of 124th Street and Fifth Avenue. Out the corner of my eye, I noticed a police officer standing on the corner. NYPD started posting officers on corners at certain locations to catch people committing motor vehicle violations. From his position, he was able to see I didn't have my seatbelt on and began to walk towards us. As I saw him approaching, I raised my left hand in a motionless wave to him, not smiling—yet presenting friendly enough, he stopped dead in his tracks, and we were able to pull off without a ticket being issued. It may have been the gesture or perhaps he caught sight of my PBA sticker, either way, after we pulled off, I took my coat off and put my seatbelt on. It's not a stretch to think my PBA sticker gave the officer reason to ignore my obvious seatbelt violation. The rest of the day continued as planned. Marie and my mother enjoyed the show; I picked them up and dropped my Mom off at Granny's and Marie at her place in Co-op City.

My mother didn't use my services until 2006, but my father, AJ, didn't wait nearly that long. The year was 2003 and my father needed a ride to his office. After having a few different careers including bus driver and youth counselor, he decided to return to school and pursue his law degree. He struggled passing the bar exam at first, but I am proud to say he finally passed and became an attorney practicing immigration law at his office in Chinatown. The majority of his clients were people of oriental descent whose relatives were having a hard time weaving through the often confusing and misleading immigration process of the United States.

This would be the first and only time he would be in my vehicle as a paying customer. To this day I'm not sure why he called me. It was far from a regular occurrence, and in hindsight, he probably just wanted to see me. In my youth, we often clashed and were not nearly as close as we needed to be. However, whenever we saw each other in our adult years, we behaved like old friends. Unfortunately, neither of us ever made a consistent effort to seek out one another nor acted or thought with a sense of urgency to repair our relationship. We behaved as if we had forever to make things right between us, and as we all know, people don't live forever. On this day, he decided he wanted me to drive him to the office. It took us about a half an hour to get there, and he didn't use his time in the vehicle to try and lecture me as parents are often known to do. Instead, we kicked it together like two friends, with his only request being I bring my daughter, Qianna, by to visit. True to my word, that's exactly what I did on Father's Day that year. As I pulled over to double park in front of the building his office was in, my Dad turned to me and asked, "How much I owe you?" I responded nonchalantly, "Whatever you feel like paying me Pops." "It's not about what I feel like paying you," he insisted, "this isn't charity. You performed a service. I am going to pay you what the ride is worth just like I would with any other cab." "Give me twenty bucks," I said abruptly. It seemed like a nice round number to me, and I had no intention of charging my dad to begin with. AJ reached into his wallet and handed me a crisp twenty-dollar bill without a problem. "Make sure you bring Qianna by," he reminded me as he stepped out of the truck.

The trips with my parents, while not filled with excitement, were memorable nonetheless. Perhaps it is because each of them had but one trip as a passenger. After my dad, I had a couple of other family members RollwithRah much more frequently.

It was a Friday night in 2003. As usual, I was in the streets, grinding to make my quota of $200 for the night. Around 7 PM, just as I was beginning to see some real progress, my cell phone rang. My younger brother, Kevin, in his distinguishable voice and cadence shot through the other end, "What's up Rah? What's going on man? Can you come and pick a brother up?" "I can't Kev. It's Friday night and I have to get this money up. I don't have time for games right now." The reply was cold but honest. I was just getting going and didn't have time to kick it. Kevin, obviously offended at the remark, shot back, "This ain't no game man. I got places to go…what, my money ain't no good with you?" "Nah, it's not that Bro…" I began, and before I could go any further Kevin cut me off. "Word…well, come on over here and get me. Me and my lady are going out, and I want to ride out in style," he said confidently. Kev wasn't off the phone before I started my engine; and right after we hung up, I began the fifteen-minute ride to pick them up. Kev and his girlfriend at the time were going to dinner downtown. There was nothing extraordinary about the trip for me; all he wanted to do was smoke a blunt on the way down and kick it with his big brother. If he had to pay someone, why not his older brother?

When I started my second tour as an OJ, as you know by now, I lived in The Bronx, on the first floor of a private house with my daughter, my wife, and her daughter. Parking was terrible, so when I got the chance to rent a parking space from someone, I jumped on it. The house next to mine had space where people parked their cars. The owner was a guy named Henry, and he had enough room for about six vehicles on the property. As many people do, Henry would take his family on vacations. I was renting a parking spot from him, and he knew I was a car service. One day he asked me, "Would you mind taking me and my family to and from the airport?" Naturally, I agreed as it seemed like the perfect fit for both Henry and myself. The vehicle taking him to the airport was literally parked in his yard, so there would be no waiting for anyone to arrive. Likewise, for me, when the time came for our trip, all I had to do was go downstairs and drive to the airport. The departure went off without a hitch. They already had their bags on the porch at the agreed upon time. We loaded up the truck and cruised to Kennedy Airport, unloaded their bags and they left for vacation. I was due to come and get them in a week.

In the summer of 2003, my ex-wife and I weren't married yet, but were teetering on the brink of separation. My beautiful ex-wife was beginning to make it clear she wanted out of the relationship. Of course, I wanted to hear nothing of it and tried to spend as much time as possible with her to change her mind. I asked her to take the ride to the airport with me so that we could talk some more and try and resolve some of our many issues. We pulled up to the airport about fifteen minutes before Henry's plane was due to land. They were arriving on an international flight which meant they wouldn't be allowed out of the terminal before passing through customs. Sometimes, clearing customs is a lengthy process, other times not so much. There's no way to tell and that was one of the reasons I brought my lady along with me. If nothing else, I figured we would have plenty of time for us to talk out our issues.

Time had dragged on for about an hour, with Stephanie and me stuck in the cyclical loop of talking, arguing, and then waiting. Every fifteen minutes or so, airport security would walk up to Candy and ask me to move. Each time I would explain my passengers were waiting to clear customs, and sometimes the guard would let me stay, other times he would insist that I just drove away and came back. Another forty-five minutes had passed before I grew so tired of the waiting game, I took a walk over to the customs area to see if I could see Henry. I figured at least if I saw him, I would know he was close to coming out. The search for Henry proved pointless, he was nowhere to be seen. Disappointed, I returned to the vehicle to wait for another hour. With no sign of Henry and my patience wearing even thinner from the repetitiveness of the arguments. We had been at the airport for over two and a half hours at that point. Frustration makes people behave irrationally. Had I been focused, I would have found somewhere to park near the airport and waited for Henry as I had previously agreed. However, after a couple of hours of hearing my ex-wife's mouth while waiting for what seemed like in vain, I decided to leave and head back home to The Bronx.

I wasn't even halfway home before my phone cell phone rang with Henry's name on the display. "What's up Rah?

I'm here. Where are you? I am sorry that I couldn't call you, but they wouldn't allow me to use my cell phone inside of the customs area." Defensive and annoyed, I immediately responded, "You finally called? I waited for over two hours. I left." Henry's voice turned from weary to dismay. "You left? Come on Rah, you know how to do this. You were supposed to put the truck in the parking lot and wait. I would have paid for the parking time…oh well, fuck it, you left now. I'll catch a cab." That is exactly what he was trying to avoid by hiring me. I felt terrible. In retrospect, I screwed that job up from top to bottom, starting with me bringing my lady along. I was working and she had no business being there. Additionally, there are plenty of secluded areas around the airport used for extended waiting periods. I could have easily parked up somewhere. Finally, Henry was a person that I rented a parking space from. It would have been in my best interest to stay on good terms with him. You're supposed to take care of the people that take care of you. I didn't. If I was ever short on rent for the parking space, he was less likely to give me a grace period now. Of course, about two months later I was a bit short on cash when it was time to pay Henry for the parking spot. The month ended in the middle of the week, which was always a bit of a lean period for me; and that was of no matter to Henry, he wanted his money. If I hadn't screwed up a couple of months prior, he probably wouldn't be stressing me, but at this point, I completely understood why he had no patience with me.

It took me sitting in the street all night, waiting on calls to raise the $125 for the parking spot. Why does it seem like when you are looking for something, you can never find it? I feel like if I wasn't strapped and in need of the cash, it would have probably come with little effort. However, because I was out there desperate for the cash, it took me forever to raise it. Experience is the best teacher, right? Several lessons were learned. I never apologized for my screw up at the airport; I wasn't man enough to readily apologize back then. Things have changed now. Henry, I am sorry Bro. Make sure you give your wife my apologies as well. Thank you for everything.

To wrap up the theme of personal connections, I'm going to tell you about another ex named Nina. Nina is a member of the 1199 union which represents hospital workers in New York City. It was Christmas time 2005, and Nina needed a ride to her Christmas party in Midtown. We were in touch off and on over the years. She knew I had started a car service, so she reached out. When she called, I was happy to hear her voice. In my youthful ignorance, I began thinking she was possibly interested in reconnecting and rekindling the old flame. It turned out all she needed was a ride. I picked her up and dropped her off as planned, and at the end of the ride I tried to overcharge her. I figured she would pay me whatever I asked, especially since she was my ex. Nina, being true to her intelligent self, wasn't a fool and paid me exactly what the ride was worth.

In a conversation with her earlier this year, I explained I was more or less retired from the car service business and was writing a book about my experiences. Nina shouted with glee; the driving business could be a dangerous one. I chose to place my faith in God and the nobility of my cause, so the threat of violence never scared me. I knew she still cared a great deal for me even though we were no longer romantically involved.

I've always said, "God is protecting me. Who do I have to fear? If someone were to try and shoot me, the gun would probably jam." I felt my spirit was on a righteous mission to provide for my family and I had nothing to fear. As it turns out, not only was I able to provide for my family, but I am also fortunate enough to have escaped with a brain full of memories, and lessons learned which I can now share with the world. At the end of the day, bills still needed to be paid and whether the customers came from the base or from a random meeting in the street, the important thing was that they came. It was nice to have some normal people as customers, instead of the illegal clientele I seemed to repeatedly be bumping into. Unfortunately, hustlers are usually the only people who can afford my prices. At the time, I needed all the money that I could get my hands on.

Chapter 8:
Out of Town

Let's flash back to the last chapter, specifically the details of my first drug run to Pennsylvania with that kid, Heavy. Over the following decade, I went on to make a couple of dozen similar trips. Fortunately, the closest I ever came to getting busted was that first trip at the DUI checkpoint. However, everyone wasn't as lucky as me. Others would later perilously learn, first-hand, the dangers involved with carrying work out of state.

As of spring 2005, I had been in the business for just under three years. Candy and I had fallen into a nice little routine. Business in the city was good enough for me to stay in The Poconos from Sunday to Thursday afternoon. I needed to make at least $650 from Thursday to Saturday night just to cover my basic weekly expenses. By the grace of god, I was able to pull that off every week for about 3 years. My Saturday nights usually ended at about four or five in the morning after the club calls with me dropping my last passenger off and heading straight back to the mountains. The calls coming from the base combined with my core of regulars kept me pretty busy.

One night I was driving up Madison Avenue after dropping Foe off when B-1 crackled through the radio, "Base time is now 12:30 in the AM. I need a large unit picking up four males. "Second shout" …large unit, four males on 135 in the Bronx headed down." The call had to be worth at least thirty dollars, so I wasted no time keying up. The B-1 queried, "9-9, ten minutes?" A cracked a smile as I responded, "Copy, Copy." The B-1 responded immediately, "9-9, you're a positive…9-9 you're a positive for the males going down." I was already headed in the direction of the call. Within five minutes, I was keying up for the building numbers of my passengers. "The males are at a strip club," she answered. Driving towards the Bruckner expressway, I pulled over at the iconic strip club that used to stand there. After I came to a stop, breaking away from the crowd at the door, a small group headed towards me. They all looked to be in their twenties, and without any indication from me, they just knew I was their ride. Sometimes the dispatchers tell the callers what color unit to be on the lookout for. The four of them climbed in. One by one, in all varying shades of brown, greeting me with a "What's Up" or "What's Good?" as they settled in the seats for the ride. Their names were Show, Umar, Boo, and Q, and they were headed downtown to a lounge in The Village. During the ride downtown, they seemed like four happy-go-lucky guys out for a night of partying; but instead of hanging in a strip club throwing money, they decided mingling with some women who had their clothes on was a better option. The fun fact I later learned about this crew was they all sold different assortments of drugs in different locations. Some of them hustled in the city and some of them hustled out-of-town, but the irony was they rarely hustled together. Sometimes money will ruin a good friendship, but then the question becomes, were y'all ever really friends to begin with? They didn't start rolling weed for the ride as soon as they sat down, like many of my other passengers did. That was a nice surprise. These brothers were different. Over the course of the next year, I would get to know a little about each of them.

Q was the smallest out of the group at about 5'4" and skinny. Naturally, he had a bit of a Napoleon complex. He often used his money to project power. For example, one afternoon Q called me to come pick him up. When I pulled up to the corner, he was standing across the street from the building he hustled out of, wearing a full golfing ensemble down to the $275 Lacoste golf cleats (he made sure to tell me the price). He strutted with such confidence that, had we been on the back nine at Pebble Beach, you'd think he just hit a hole-in-one. The only problem is that we weren't walking through any lush greens where you might actually need fucking cleats. We were in the hood. Q had never played golf, yet that didn't stop him from wearing the outfit or bragging to anyone listening, that it cost him over $600. He was desperate to show that he had money to burn. Some people use material possessions for validation of character or happiness. A lot of times, they crave the attention they were deprived of growing up. Every night, he would pay me to take him on a five-minute ride to get fried shrimp and mashed potatoes from this twenty-four-hour seafood spot across the Fordham Road bridge. Q was always blowing money. One time, he asked me to take him to the barber shop about a mile away from his block. I took a nap while waiting outside for him to finish then took him back home. The roundtrip took three hours. Q paid me ninety dollars for what would have been only a fifteen-dollar cab ride. Later, he joked, "That's the most expensive haircut that I ever got!"

Show wasn't that type of person. He often spoke about hustling not being a career as much as it was a means to an end. When he found out that I owned property in the mountains, he began to ask me about investments and different potential joint business ventures. Show was raised in the South. He didn't see himself in the crab barrel as most of the hood did. He was open to the possibilities of more.

Boo was the muscle of the group. He had done a couple bids, and like most inmates in jail, he spent a lot of it lifting weights. From what I could see from my time with him, he wasn't much in the brains department, but I'm probably biased because I've seen him smoke angel dust. Nonetheless, he was a cool dude who never got out of line or tried to disrespect me, so we got along fine.

Umar, for some odd reason thought it would be funny if he started calling me Porkchop. I told him that I don't even eat pork, and he kept calling me that, so it never made sense. Maybe it was him trying to bust my chops? He was laid back and carefree, but surprisingly cheap. Once, he wanted me to take him out of town to where he hustled. It didn't happen because according to him, my price was too high. After that first trip out of town, I knew if I was going back, it needed to be worth it. Otherwise, the only time I ever saw him was with one of the others.

They all had different ways of making moves, but on this first night, they were just four dudes I was taking downtown. It took hardly any time before we were pulling up at the location. Q was sitting in the front and doing most of the talking on the ride down. I should have known the type of guy he would turn out to be. Even though we had been speaking, he just hopped out of the truck without exchanging salutations. No big deal: it wasn't like I was trying to be his friend. The other three in the back soon followed suit, hopped out and headed straight down the steps into the lounge. Show happened to be the last person getting out, so I shouted to him, "Yo! You guys haven't paid yet!" He tried to call his other friends so that they could chip in, but they kept going. Looking back, it was probably their custom to not be the last person out the cab so that you didn't get caught having to pay for it.

Show turned back around and walked back towards Candy's passenger window. I had a suspicion there wasn't a plan in place for them to get back uptown, and Show confirmed it when he said, "Damn, I don't know if they want you to wait or what." Waiting wasn't an option, and I didn't have to say a word before Show quickly read my expression and continued, "Forget it, yo. How much we owe you?" "Thirty dollars," I answered. Show reached into his left pocket and pulled out a stack of cash, peeling off thirty dollars, and turned to go back in the lounge. He wasn't able to take two steps before I shouted after him, "Yo! Take my number just in case." I knew they didn't have a way back up, so I decided to mill around the area. It is not like I had anywhere in particular to go. My gut said they would be in the spot for an hour at the max. The spots downtown have different patrons than hood bars, and in most instances, hood dudes at classy spots downtown, don't get much love from the ladies. Just over forty minutes passed before Show rang my phone asking, "How long would it take for you to swing around and pick us up?" "Give me about fifteen minutes, I'll be there," I responded. In all honesty I could have been there in Two minutes. I didn't want it to seem like I was thirsty or just sitting around twiddling my thumbs, so I said, "Fifteen minutes". I drove the three blocks back to the lounge only to find them already standing outside. They climbed back into Candy and gave me the addresses for their drop offs. Show was going to his apartment in the building he shared with his mother on Burnside Avenue. Boo and Q were about a mile away from Show's apartment, with Umar living the furthest away. He wanted to be dropped off uptown at his parents' house off East Gun Hill Road. By the time I dropped everyone off, I had exchanged phone numbers with all of them and collected a total of $80 dollars over the course of two hours.

As the weeks wore on, I dealt with different members of the crew at different times. My first encounter was with Q as I mentioned, picking him up would become a nightly occurrence to go to his favorite seafood restaurant and get fried shrimp and mashed potatoes. I arrived at the same location I previously dropped him and Boo off at. Q approached Candy from the passenger window and said, "I am taking care of some business inside, but I want you to wait. So don't worry, you are on the clock starting now. I got you."

As it turns out Q was only going to meet up with Show, and what would have been an $8 ride, ended up being $40, because he had me wait around. He clearly had no concept of the value of money outside of it buying the stuff he wanted. I wasn't going to complain though, if not for people like Q, I wouldn't have survived for all of those years doing what I did. We pulled up on the corner of Show's block to find there were no parking spaces, so I stopped at the fire hydrant. Within a few minutes, Show came downstairs with a friend of his walking behind him. He introduced him with a quick, "Rah, this is Boogs," and the four of us were off. They wanted to go to another strip club, one different from the one I picked them up at, and coincidentally they wanted to go to the same spot that I had taken Foe to, where my homeboy Deezo was the DJ. I always got in free on the strength of Deezo, so I decided to stay and kick it with my new passengers to see what they were really all about.

Most of our time inside the club was spent focusing on the half-naked women walking around the spot. We got a table in the corner, Show and Boogs went halves on a bottle of vodka which normally cost you $30 in the liquor store but sold for $150 inside of the club. As they reached in their pockets and peeled off cash for the bottle, I instantly realized the wad of cash Show pulled out to pay me with before wasn't a one-off instance; and I needed to be charging more because these dudes obviously had money to blow.

We were in the club for no more than three hours. On the way home, Show recommended I drop Q off first, since Show and Boogs were headed to the same spot. When we got over to University Avenue, Q hopped out and disappeared into his building; we continued the short mile trip to Show's building. This is when he explained that he Boogs sold drugs just like his other boys, but they didn't waste time with it in the city. "Rah we've been up in Vermont getting at that paper…you feel me?" I was doing the calculations in my head. Show was serious when he talked, and on the two separate instances he pulled those huge wads of cash, you could tell it wasn't a display of arrogance like Q's. It was just how he moved. I immediately began thinking about how much would I charge to go all the way up to Vermont. It was basically a five-hundred-mile round trip from the city. Numbers and calculations began whizzing in my brain, but before I got too far in my thoughts, Show brought me back to reality. "We need somebody to take us up to Albany," he said. "From there, we got a old dude meeting us at the bus station to take us the rest of the way to Vermont. What I'm tryna figure out is how much Rah?" My mind flashed back to my last out of town trip. "Three hundred bucks," casually rolled off my tongue. Show and Boogs looked at each other. They both knew that, If they wanted somebody cool and low risk to take them, they were going to have to pay for it. "Cool," said Show quietly. "We can do that."

Walking away with my freedom from those runs Mike had previously set up had emboldened me. In my mind, I didn't see it as breaking the law, even though I know it most certainly was. On the contrary, I viewed myself as a crusader, trying to survive in an economy which had kicked me and others to the curb. After making moves to Pennsylvania, and helping to move that white powder, I felt untouchable to the point I didn't bother asking Show what they were carrying. When you first meet a person, they never come straight out and say, "I want you to take me out of town with some drugs." On the flip side to that, as a driver, you don't agree to take just anybody out of town because any stupid moves or mistakes by anyone riding in the vehicle, is typically enough to cost everyone riding in the vehicle their freedom. At this point we had spent the last couple of days around each other, including our time in the strip club, so we both felt comfortable enough to make the trip. A large part of Show's character was him being raised in the South and having the demeanor associated with having done a hard day's work in the yard. Even though our time together was brief, I felt I could trust Show. "We'll be ready to go early in the morning so if you want to crash, you can."

I regularly slept in the truck so that I could catch calls all night but the idea of sleeping on a couch at my new homeboy Show's crib to get to the money the next day worked for me. I knew from overhearing their other conversations, all they liked to do was smoke and play video games. They seemed harmless enough to me. My instincts were correct. I took the run up to Albany maybe four or five times to drop them off with each time seeming easier than the previous. As long as I did the speed limit or even slightly above, and didn't do anything to draw attention to myself, it was practically impossible to get caught.

One night before going on one of those runs upstate, the boys hit the town for a last bit of New York fun. They didn't call me to drive them around, so I had no idea what was going on. What I do know is, Show rang my phone the next morning much earlier than he was supposed to. We made plans to head upstate around noon. It was just before 9:45 AM when I answered the phone to hear Show say, "Yo Rah, Morning. I bagged this chick last night. I need you to drop her off in Jersey before we bust that move." A trip to Jersey on a Saturday morning is not what I had in mind for breakfast. I had only walked through my door from a busy Friday night no more than four hours earlier, and I was hoping to catch a few more winks before hitting the road. "Son…," I said in disbelief. He heard my tone, and quickly added, "Shorty lives right across the bridge…she's not deep in Jerz." That was a relief. "Okay. I'm gonna get myself together, I'll call you when I'm outside," I replied. "Give me like an hour." I lumbered out of the bed and into the shower. Almost exactly one hour later, I was calling Show and telling him to send the chick downstairs. Just as Show had said, the girl lived about ten minutes into Jersey so dropping her off wasn't a problem.

The problem came on my return trip to New York. I got back onto that section of I-95 North and wound up in the express lanes headed towards the George Washington Bridge. On this Saturday morning and most mornings, those lanes were packed with traffic. As we creeped along in traffic, I saw a break in the median dividing the express and local lanes. The break is reserved for emergency vehicles. At that moment I felt that it was an emergency I got out of that traffic. At first, I was hesitant to use the break, but when I saw two and then three vehicles do it, my attitude turned from reluctant, to "Fuck it." As soon as I completely crossed over into the local lanes, a State Trooper came swooping onto the highway. He came down a ramp from his elevated position. He couldn't have been sitting there the whole time, or else he would have pulled over the first several drivers who went before me; I was simply unlucky. He ended up pulling up alongside my vehicle with his sirens blaring and shouted as he pointed to me, "Follow me! You better follow me!" I had no choice but to listen. I knew that if I didn't " obey his orders", he was going to radio ahead and have one of his partners give me two tickets, at the least, barring they didn't arrest me for evading an officer. I followed him for about one hundred yards until he was able to pull over the other vehicle he was chasing. We both got $140 tickets that day. I made my way back to the city to pick up Show and

Boogs for our scheduled trip upstate. When I told Show I got pulled over and got a ticket his response was, "Don't worry about it, Rah. Just add it to the tab."

Over that year, I learned Show and Boogs dealt almost exclusively with cocaine. Cocaine made people a lot of money and was the party drug of choice for some. For others, sometimes the rush of coke was too powerful for them, and when that happened, they would look to Oxycodone for relief. Oxycodone is part of the opiate family and counters the effects of cocaine. One day Show and I were talking when he said, "I got custies up in Vermont that would be willing to pay as much as $100 for one Oxy pill. If you could somehow get your hands on some, we can easily make ten or twelve thousand dollars in a matter of a week to ten days." My brain did a somersault at the idea of twelve racks in ten days. The only thing I felt like I needed, was extra capital. Disposable income would mean the sky was truly the limit. I immediately began to look around for a connect for us because finding one would make me a partner, which would also grant me a larger portion of return.

I dealt with so many people, it was only a matter of time before someone would point me in the right direction and sure enough around February 2005, it happened. One day I picked up a call from 115th Street and Malcolm X Boulevard. Old school Harlem folks still call it Lenox Avenue. Four guys in their mid-twenties climbed into Candy for an hour hold to make a few stops in the hood. During the ride, I asked if they knew where I would be able to find some Oxys.

There was a taller, heavy-set caramel-skinned dude sitting in the rear passenger seat. His most memorable feature was his size and the Turquoise Florida Marlins baseball cap that he wore on his head. Bright colors make you too identifiable to either rivals or authorities. He was quick to speak up and say, "I can get those for you. I know what you are talking about."

Based on a talk I previously had with Show, I knew there were different strengths based on the number of milligrams associated with each pill, and each milligram was a different color. The weakest being an Oxy 5 which pretty much resembled a Bayer Aspirin with its off-white coloring. The 30s, were more sky blue. We were looking for the top of the line—the most potent and most destructive Oxycontin, the 80 mg mint green, which was easy enough to remember because green is the color of money. When I asked which ones he had, Mr. Marlin scoffed with a smirk and said, "I got those 80's…There's an old man on my floor who has the script for them. He likes to get high, so I trade him the Oxys for Crack." "Word. I'm going to talk to my guy. What's the numbers?" I asked. "Well shit, it's all profit for me…twenty-five a pill," he replied. At this point we were pulling up to their destination, but I knew the universe put them in my truck for this reason. It was too perfect. "Word up. Well, we're here," I said as I shifted Candy into park. "I'm going to hit my dude and get in touch with you in a bit if it's a go." "Bet," he said as the three of them stepped out of Candy and disappeared into a building.

I knew Show was going to jump all over the deal since it was exactly what we were looking for. On the way back uptown, I called Show. "Yo Show, I got some good news. I found a connect, he wants twenty-five a pill." "Oh, word? That's love. Hell, Yeah Rah! That's a go. Tell the kid I am coming through to cop a hundred of those things…Come and get me," he exclaimed. "Cool. Give me a little bit, I'll be there in a second," I replied. We hung up, and I began to make my way to The Bronx. By spending $2,500 in Harlem, Show could turn around and easily make $10,000 up in Vermont. That is not a bad profit for less than a week's worth of work.

After picking up Show from his apartment in the Bronx, we were on our way back to Harlem within an hour or so. As we got closer, I gave Mr. Marlin a call to let him know to meet me in front of his building so that he and my boy could handle their business. I always made sure to try to stay in the truck when drug transactions were taking place, because if the cops ever showed up, I would be nowhere to be found. True to his word, Mr. Marlin was standing in front of his building when we pulled up. Show unbuckled his seatbelt, hopped out the car and just that fast, him and Mr. Marlin disappeared into the building. It wasn't any longer than maybe five minutes when Show returned to Candy. As he opened the passenger door and climbed in, "We good?" I asked enthusiastically. "No," he said. His tone was sullen, and his head was down. It was difficult to read, but the obvious read was things didn't go as planned. "No…let's be out." I glanced over his shoulder to see Mr. Marlin had reemerged from the building and taken his usual post in front. I jumped out of Candy step to him and see what had gone wrong. I didn't like the idea of him wasting me and my homeboy's time on what now appeared to be a wild goose chase. I was no more than two steps away from the car door when Show swung open the passenger door and yelled, "Yo! Get back in the truck Rah! Yo Rah! Get back in the truck!" Show and I had a good relationship. It was extremely unusual for him to speak so forcefully to me. I figured that it would be best to listen. He obviously knew something I didn't. I took one longer look at Mr. Marlin, then turned around and opened the car door to climb back in Candy.

About five blocks later, Show began to explain what happened after they got in the building. "So, me and dude walk into the building, and I'm not thinking shit of it, we walk to the stairwell and dude looks at me and says, 'Yo, you look familiar. You live around here, or you be around here or something?'. So, I tell him, my cousin lives across the street. I've never seen this nigga ever, Rah. So, I tell him who my cousin is, and he says, 'If it wasn't for your cousin being one of my niggas from the hood and a killer on top of that, I would have robbed your ass. You can't be walking in here like this with that much cash on you. I am going to tell your cousin you're out here fucking up.'…But the mindfuck is Rah…I've never seen this nigga before in my life!" My mind was blown. Of all the possible outcomes, what had just transpired wasn't even on the list. Show stopped me from confronting Mr. Marlin when I got out of the truck because he knew that the kid had a gun on him. I was pissed Mr. Marlin tried to use me to set my boy up. Looking back at it, Show probably saved my life that day. If a dude was down to rob somebody in his building stairwell with a gun, he probably wouldn't have thought twice about pumping a few bullets into some cab driver he had just met. That was my bad. I would never purposely put Show in harm's way, and he never held it against me. Simply put, he knew I was caught out there just like he almost was.

Like most drug dealers, the law eventually caught up to Show's partner, Boogs, and he was arrested and had to go to jail to serve about two years. His partner being caught meant the cops could be closer than he thought. We fell out of touch when Show decided it was wise to fall back for a minute. He resurfaced a couple of years later, with a random call out of the blue saying he needed to talk about something face-to-face. I already knew it was about something illegal because most things could be said over the phone. I agreed to meet him and pulled up on his block while he was out walking his pit bull. He was wearing a dark hoodie with the hood drawn over his head—a tactic he used to hide the swollen, bruised lump he was sporting, over his right eye. He explained he was no longer working out of town and had resorted to hustling and getting money from local sales in his hood. The thing was, the entire time Show was making moves out of town, there were guys selling drugs in his hood, that didn't welcome him with open arms. "Rah, I need to get this nigga out of here. You know a hitter? Just tell me how much, and I'll put the bread up." As it turned out, I knew a pack of BLOODs about five blocks away who would have loved to put some work in, but I didn't want any blood on my hands. Even if I wasn't pulling the trigger myself, I knew in some shape or form, I would be responsible for someone getting killed. I also didn't want any of the homies from around the corner to get arrested and sent to jail based upon a lead that I gave them. There was a brief silence between Show asking me, and me finally responding, "Nah, I don't even know anybody, Show. My bad..." "It's cool. I figured I'd ask you because you know so many people. Also, I know I can trust you." I was trusting myself to keep my homie's out of trouble. By now it should be no secret, I am afraid of that bitch, Karma, and I try to tread on the right side of her.

I caught up with the homies I would have hit up for the job a few days later. At this point, there was no potential chance of them getting the hit, at least not through me, so I told them about it. One of them said, "Yo Rah, you should have called us! We have plenty of cats we can use to get that done. That would've been light work." It was never a doubt whether they could've got the job done; I always knew they could. I also knew I didn't want that shit on my conscience if anything went wrong. I never heard from Show again after that meeting. I hope nothing crazy happened to him. I still remember where his mother lives. Maybe I should pass through one day to see how my boy is doing. I learned a lot by watching and driving Show around on those runs out of town. Those trips were some of my first out of town runs. Just because Show wasn't in the car anymore, didn't mean I wasn't going back out of town.

Observing the local speed limit, is number one on a short list of rules to stick to, while riding dirty out of town. It's important to stay within the flow of traffic. Driving too slow may arouse the same amount of suspicion as driving too fast would; if not more. The second rule is stay sober--that goes for weed and alcohol. Apart from the obvious danger of driving under the influence, a cop that smells alcohol becomes suspicious. The last thing that you want to do is to give those fuckers a reason. Remember that DUI checkpoint we ran into on my first trip out of town? The officer had no probable cause to search the vehicle because I was obviously sober. How do you think that same interaction would go if I had a beer or two before the trip, and he caught a faint whiff of alcohol on my breath?

Most of the runs I made took place in the middle of the night and required me to persevere through adverse driving conditions, especially fatigue. No matter how tired I got, I always followed rule number three: don't stay overnight. Running someone out of town almost always implied unfamiliar territory. What if the stash house has nosy neighbors that were watching the house, waiting for the chance to snitch? What if whoever you were taking had beef, and the other person was waiting for their return? It's easy to get caught up in bullshit by being seen with the wrong person. History is littered with stories of being in the wrong place at the wrong time. The easiest way to limit the chance of that occurring is by making the drop and rolling out. In the worst-case scenario, it was always wiser to leave the town and stop at the first gas station or rest stop on the highway to sleep.

One of the major keys to successfully making runs repeatedly was never allowing my face to become too familiar with the people out of town, so my fourth rule was remaining unfamiliar, and don't be seen. The less people knew, the better. The only thing people ever saw was an inconspicuous Candy barreling down the highway.

The drug trade was built on supply and demand, not promises and IOUs. It was dangerous business to be transporting, and fortunately for me, sales didn't need to be made for me to get my cut. Rule number five: when possible, collect the money up front. The easiest way to collect up front, especially if it's your first time with a new associate, would be to ask for at least half of the total fee for gas and tolls. Positioning the payment as a trip expense instead of saying, "I need half up front because I don't know or trust you…" is always easier and better for business.

Sticking to the rules is the difference between jail and freedom, or even worse, life and death. Some people break the rules and don't talk about it because they escaped safely and value their freedom. Some people break the rules and live to tell the story, albeit from a prison visiting room, the story is still heard. People have spent the duration of their lives in prison cells for less, so it doesn't take much to go from driver of your own vehicle to suspect in the back of a police car, especially when you're " riding dirty". I've been in some sticky situations before, and more than one of them revolved around, one particular figure named Fat Boy.

Flashback to 2004, when I was stressed by a crumbling relationship, uninspired, and didn't want to do much of anything other than sit around feeling sorry for myself. My younger brother, Kevin, recognized the distress signals and took it upon himself to ride with me to try and keep my spirits up. We were in the clear as long as it was a daytime, riding double at night was prohibited. One afternoon, we were in Harlem when we heard a call to pick up two males from the Eastside of Manhattan.

The dispatcher told me that the two males were requesting a slight hold, which would've lasted about half an hour. When we pulled up to the spot, a heavy-set, bowlegged guy in his mid-to-late twenties sauntered over to Candy. Fat Boy was closely followed by a much slimmer brown-skin guy who looked to be about the same age. They climbed into the second row and began directing me around Harlem to make their stops. Every stop was within a one-mile radius, so we didn't even leave the Eastside. Nothing special happened during this first call, it was just a fat dude and his homeboy making stops, with no indication of what would come down the line. He stopped by a couple of stores on Third Avenue to window shop, and then breezed by to check one of his homies for a minute. All together, we were out for about forty-five minutes before Fat Boy asked me to head back to where I picked them up, to drop them off. Just like everyone else, he asked for my number just in case he needed a ride, and then they got out.

Fat Boy had plenty of aliases and the business to match. Over the course of the next few months, he popped in and out of town; and whenever he was in town, Tone (perhaps his most popular alias) hired me exclusively as his driver. Sometimes I would be called upon to shuttle his dear old mother around and other times it would be him on the move, or him with one of his lady friends. After a while, he began to view me as his right hand. He once told me, "The first time I saw that big black bitch coming around the corner, I knew that I had to get inside of her." Did he just call my girl Candy a bitch? I always thought the statement was weird, but I appreciated the enthusiasm. I worked hard to keep her in the shape she was in.

Most of the time, he used the time we spent riding through different hoods bragging to me about his violent past. In the months prior to us meeting, Tone had just got home from prison after beating a murder charge. He was charged and

219

incarcerated in a state penitentiary while his case was under appeal for three years. Because of his prior criminal record, was denied bail and had to stay locked up while his case was on appeal. The story went Tone and some other dude in Harlem had some sort of beef which grew to the point each of them had begun carrying a weapon just in case they bumped into one another. One day, Tone was riding with an OJ across 119th Street. As they pull up to the corner of Adam Clayton Powell, Tone spotted his target standing with three other men. He never noticed Tone at the light. While waiting for the light to turn green, one of the dudes standing by Tone's enemy noticed Tone in the car and immediately pointed him out. They must have thought it was a drive by because homie turned around shooting at the car. The fear of being vulnerable inside of the car, charged through Tone as he hopped out and took cover behind the engine block and started returning fire. The light turned green, and the OJ sped off leaving Tone coverless with adrenaline pumping through his veins, he hit his target with three shots center mass. Tone told me that his mother had spent over fifty-thousand dollars in lawyer fees and appeals for him to beat the case. Eventually the lawyers got his conviction overturned on the grounds of self-defense, on grounds the other guy fired first, and Tone had no choice but to fire back. The three years he sat during the appeal process counted as time served, and he was released. He often boasted about that incident. Tone proudly claimed that him and his shenanigans were the reason, security cameras were installed in all of the project grounds.

I had been Tone's main driver for quite a while. Naturally , when it was time for his brother to make a run out of town, he relied on me. It was around May 2004 when Tone called me, "Yo Rah, what's good?" "I'm chillin…making some moves. What's up?" I responded. "Yo, I need a favor. How much would you charge me to run up to Massachusetts?" he asked. I had never been that far up, so I never even thought about it. "It's only a few hours away," he added. Tone had been giving me so much business, I figured I would give him a bit of a discount. "Give me two hundred bucks," I said nonchalantly. "When you trying to go?" "Today, like tonight," he answered. "For real, for real…can you come get me now? Two hundred is love." "Yeah, I can be on my way. It's no big deal, I'll see you in a little bit bro," I replied. "Okay, bet!" he said excitedly before hanging up. I had never been to Massachusetts on a run like this, but I was sure that I'd be fine. By the time I parked on Tone's block, Tone, his brother, and the white chick his brother was dating at the time were waiting outside. They walked up to Candy single-file—Tone climbed in the front seat and his brother opened the door for the white lady to hop in the back seat first. On one of the various runs around the city, Tone had already mentioned he would occasionally head OT (out of town) his brother to handle some business. As they clicked their seatbelts and I shifted Candy into drive, Tone said, "Yo Rah, I appreciate it. Don't worry either, we're just dropping him off…it's not like a run or anything like that." I appreciated him reassuring me, but I knew there was no way for me to know if they actually had anything on them, nor did I want to know. The less details, the better. That first ride to Massachusetts was uneventful, and Tone's brother didn't like me for my no cigarettes rule. Once we got to Massachusetts, they were supposed to meet someone at the train station but whoever that was never showed up, which prompted him to ask me to take him further in town. I agreed to do so for an additional fee out of principle. We had driven all that way, I obviously wasn't going to leave him stranded but the fact remained we agreed on a destination, which now had changed.

I dropped Tone's brother and his girlfriend off and began the trip back home. "You know my brother has this whole shit on smash up here…," Tone began. "…like all this shit, bro." "That's crazy," I replied. "They don't ever get nervous about being all the way out here in the burbs. It's a lot of white people up here son…" Tone laughed, "It's mad white people. What's even crazier…," he paused in between chuckles, "…is that the white girl we just dropped off is the mayors' daughter, and that the cops won't arrest my bro, off the strength! This shit is sweet up here for real, Rah." As much as I believed that his brother had some sort of immunity for screwing the mayor's daughter, it turned out to be false. A few years later his brother got five years after getting arrested in that same town. Who knows, maybe he did have immunity for a few years, and it ran out?

As we were driving towards the highway, we passed two police cars driving towards us. I didn't think look for them after we passed them, but about a mile after passing them, I saw the flashing red and blue lights as they signaled to pull us over. I pulled over to the shoulder and turned the radio down, unsure of what to expect. We were a ways off from the highway and everything around us was dimly lit to darkness, with the exception of the faint orange from the streetlights that appeared about every one hundred yards. The spotlight on the police car flicked on and reflected off of my sideview mirror and temporarily blinded me. As my eyes adjusted to the white glare of the lamp, I looked away and waited patiently for someone to approach my window. I had heard the stories about how wicked county police could be. Tone was on probation. Any contact with law enforcement would be an excuse for him to be violated by his probation officer. Additionally, a condition of any prisoner's parole release or probation monitoring is not leaving the five boroughs of New York City without permission. I had to play it cool. Anything deemed as mouthing off to the cops would give them all the probable cause they needed to harass us further and maybe arrestTone for being out of the state.

The first cop to approach the car was a clean- shaven white man, somewhere in his early thirties. Another officer who looked older in stature and appearance, slowly exited his car and waddled up behind and towards the passenger side where Tone was sitting. "Good morning," I began, "what seems to be the problem, officer?" "Morning…well, I pulled you over because your high beams were on, and you failed to dim them as you approached our vehicle. License and registration, please?" he asked. The other officer watched the vehicle and interaction without speaking. He was right. I didn't dim my high beams as we passed their cars, but it was dark, and it was only for a moment. The reason seemed trivial, which let me know that these were the type of cops to abuse power if they wanted to, and that was even more reason to stay cool. "Sure, I'm just going to reach into my glove compartment and grab my registration and insurance card," I said to the officer. I reached over Tone to open the glove compartment and pulled out the envelope with the papers and handed it over to the cop with my license. "Thanks, I'll be right back." He turned around and started the ten foot walk back to his car door, with the other officer reconvening with him at his window. We sat in the car quietly, for two minutes while the officer began radioing in my information to check for any known aspects of criminality.

"What a crock of shit…," I said to Tone, while I watched the officer begin what looked like him writing a ticket. "Fuckin, high beams son…." Tone didn't seem phased, but he also didn't acknowledge the statement. I'm sure he was partially panicked by the thought of being arrested out of state, so he stayed quiet and still as to not draw any unnecessary attention. Another five minutes passed before I saw the police car door swing open and the officer step out and start his walk back to my window. "Okay, so here's your paperwork and license, and I wrote you a ticket for your headlights not working properly. It can be dismissed at any local precinct… bring the ticket, the officer will come out and check the headlights and dismiss it. You guys are free to go, have a good day." The older officer didn't even bother making the trip back to Candy for the ticket issuing. I knew the ticket was bullshit, and even though Tone told me him and his brother were clean, there was no way that I could know for sure, so I thanked God we were headed back to New York and not jail.

My brother, Kevin, witnessed firsthand the handfuls of money I made with ease while doing my job. He spent a decent amount of time riding double with me, to the point, one day he told me he wanted to try being an OJ. I was always down to put my brother onto some money, so that winter in 2005, I took Kevin to the Chevrolet dealership in The Poconos where he ended up leasing a 2003 Tahoe. I thought it was fitting that my little brother got a smaller version of my truck, which he named Bruno. I wasn't on the streets by myself anymore. I had my little brother who I could throw some calls when things got too busy for me to handle. I tried explaining the nuances and unwritten rules of being an OJ to Kevin. I feel like if Baby Bro would have listened to me he would have saved himself a lot of hassles down the line.

Kevin spent the entire summer of 2004 in the hospital with a severe digestive system issue that nearly killed him. As a result, he became regularly fatigued and psychologically traumatized. Before getting sick, Kevin worked a regular job and sold weed on the side. He loves money so he was always working to the point he got a tattoo self-proclaiming himself "The twenty-five Hour hustler." After he got out of the hospital, Kevin's appetite for money stayed consistent, but he didn't have the stamina to rip and run like he used to. Towards the end of the summer, Tone approached me and asked me to take him and his crew to Pennsylvania.

In full transparency, if it was Tone by himself, I would have done it. However, Tone's crew consisted of a couple of guys I didn't care for. Based on their negative vibe I refused to down to do the trip. By this point in time, Kevin and Tone had developed a friendship rooted in quite a few commonalities. They were both aspiring rappers who were also heavy weed smokers. They spent hours-on end talking about music and weed. Foe kept me pretty busy, so Kevin usually went to pick up Tone when I was unavailable. So of course, when I refused the request to go to Pennsylvania, Kevin accepted.

The regular path of an OJ usually involves time in the streets and learning the ropes. In most industries, there isn't a way around apprenticeship—it's a fundamental part of the process. Kevin simply saw the dollar amount. He wasn't there for the tough lessons or precarious situations that birthed my career. He wanted and tried to be a driver, but driving wasn't the type of work everyone could do. Unfortunately, it was a too late in the game when he realized the job was tougher than it looked. A new truck meant he now had a car note in addition to the other bills he was already paying. Naturally, he jumped at the chance to take Fat Boy and his crew out of town. When he told me he was thinking about doing the run, one of the things I said to him was, "Baby Bro…remember, there are rules to this shit." He was pressed for cash, so I could understand why he was thinking about the trip. I never explicitly told him not to make the run—I don't think I could ever tell another grown man not to go make money. I never explicitly said, "I'm not going because I don't like the vibes of the crew." We both knew the group that Fat Boy had around him were a bunch of clowns.

The trip was to the town Sunbury, a small mountain town about 160 miles from New York City. Several months prior, Tone had a friend head out to Sunbury to set up shop and secure a place to stay. As he started to feel comfortable, he slowly invited more of his friends down to get in on the game. Typically, in these situations, things go relatively well in the beginning. It takes a while for small towns to catch on to what is going on because deals happen behind closed doors, and you must know who to ask to find them. Outside of the normal pleasantries, people usually keep to themselves. The cocaine business in Sunbury was going so well, some of the crew decided to expand the market to other drugs heroin. That decision would prove fatal.

When a few of the local high school kids died from an overdose, it went from a good time getting money to State of Emergency, fast. Both State and Federal agencies got involved to assist the local authorities with tracking down the source of the problem. In fact, most problems don't find rapid solutions until suburban white kids are affected. When kids start dying, it's time to get that shit off the street. As if kids dying from their heroin wasn't enough, members in the crew also started selling illegal firearms. Typically, illegal guns go to people that can't buy legal ones. Those people usually use those illegal guns to commit crimes, and gun crimes are every suburban town's nightmare. The DEA and FBI were tracking the source of the heroin overdoses when the ATF began their investigations for the sudden spurt in gun violence.

Neither Tone, my brother or myself knew any of this before they went down there. For Kevin, Sunbury was a place he could lay low and sell weed while still getting money for helping Tone. Tone was in Sunbury to hustle up cash and head back to New York and continue to provide for his family. Neither of them had direct involvement with the rest of the dudes or the mess they were creating down there. During the trial, Chad, Kevin's arresting ATF agent, said to me "Kevin had to be the unluckiest person in the world." He explained how the investigation was in the final stages when Kevin and Tone showed up for the first time. They were spotted by the agent running surveillance in a bread truck up the block from where they were staying. When Kevin got to Sunbury, Tone persuaded him to stay with him for a while. Tone needed a way to get to the customers and Kevin was in no hurry to get back to New York, so it made sense. In return, Tone offered him a share of the profits from the cocaine sales and Kevin would be able to sell his weed freely and keep the profits. Sunbury is about fifty minutes away from my house in The Poconos. I always told my brother, "People come to Pennsylvania to live and vacation, not to sell drugs. Once he told me that he was staying out there, I reminded him of the rules which I shared with him before he even started in the business.

Ultimately my brother was convicted of conspiracy to distribute an excess of fifty grams of crack cocaine for the four trips he made between New York and Sunbury. That is exactly half the amount I took out of town with me on the first run Mike had set up for me. Grand total, the month Kevin spent with the crew in Sunbury earned him five years at the prison work camp in Lewisburg, Pennsylvania. Fortunately, he only served a little less than three years in custody. Tone also went to prison, along with roughly sixteen other people. Strangely enough Tone came home before my brother. Tone, the man who led Kev to Sunbury and into all of that bullshit, served less time than my brother. I never blamed Fat Boy, but the facts are what they are. I felt guilty because he got in the business trying to follow in my footsteps. I felt guilty because I introduced him to Tone, who ultimately got him introduced to prison. Until his release, I wouldn't leave a tour of duty in New York without making sure I made an extra $50 to put into his commissary account. As time passed I got over my feeling of guilt. He had said it himself several times over, "He made his own choice."

Fast forward to the year October 2009, two years after my brother's conviction, Tone's mother called me for a ride. She was on 125th Street in Harlem and wanted to go to Central Avenue in Yonkers. That was easily a $50 call, at minimum, so I made my way to her without wasting any time. I pulled up to find her sitting with two young adults, a man and woman, somewhere between the ages of twenty to twenty-five. Eventually I learned the young man, Freddy B, was one of her foster children and he had a kid with the girl they were traveling with. Apparently, they were on their way to the UGGs boot store. The ride took around twenty-five minutes. Freddy used the time to let me know he had heard a lot of good things about me. He seized the opportunity to propose several hypothetical scenarios and asked the legal ramifications of each scenario. I welcomed the opportunity to display my knowledge, and I was flattered he was looking to me for answers, but little did I know, Freddy B was interviewing me.

We dropped the ladies off at the UGGs store, and Freddy asked me to take him to the liquor store on 139th Street and Lenox Avenue so we could talk. There I found out he was following in what could be considered the family business, selling drugs, with the only difference between operations being Freddy was a one-man show. He was hustling in the same small town in Massachusetts where I had dropped his brother off a few years prior, and he was asking me to take him up there. "Yo Rah, listen…I'm gonna need you to take me up to Mass on my next run, if you could. How much would you charge me?" he asked. "I've been going back and forth all this time. I usually would get a fiend to pick me up or some shit…I ain't really tryna fuck with that if I don't have to. It's risky, you feel me?" I did feel him. That was extra risky. A drug fiend is loyal to no one but the demon that fuels their addiction. They can and will turn on you in a moment's notice. "You know…," he continued, "in a perfect world, you could stay up there with me for a bit and get some money yourself." "I'm good on that," I replied . "I can take you on that next run, no problem though." "You sure? It can be a real good situation if you play it right," he said convincingly. I knew driving him up there wouldn't be an issue because driving is what I did, and I knew I was blessed after surviving everything I had; fear no longer lived in my heart. I could go and make some extra bread, but a huge part of my blessings is because I make the deliberate choice to not make bad decisions. "We'll see…but I can definitely take you though," I said again.

When the day came to take the trip, I knew what he had in mind. I had already gone over the pros and cons of being out of town for an extended period of time. Even though it was breaking the rules I decided it could be done. Before the trip, I did some research on the town. The place we were headed was in The Berkshires. I used the internet to look up the size of the town and the size of their police force. The resources available at any town's disposal are a metric I used to calculate the risk of staying. Researching showed me The Berkshires were very much like The Poconos; it was a collection of towns instead of just one small town. Like The Poconos, their economy was tourism based, offering a variety of lodges and resorts for winter sports. This would help me blend in. Pennsylvania plates made it easy for local law enforcement to write me off as a tourist in the event we were ever spotted.

The ride up took about two and a half hours, so I used the time to interview Freddy. Irony would've been if I were to get arrested dealing with Freddy when my brother was serving time because of his dealings with Tone. On the way up, I asked about everything I could think of regarding our trip. After a while Freddy grew tired of my questions and sharply said, "Wait until you see how it is up there…it's sweet. Chill, Bro." Freddy wasn't lying. We never even so much as caught an awkward gaze from the cops, but to say things were as smooth as a summer vacation would be inaccurate. There were plenty of other obstacles we had to overcome and fortunately for me, I was well prepared.

Freddy was renting out the first floor in a weather-beaten house owned by the mother of one of his smokers. The house hadn't been maintained over the years, and both the carpeting and furniture were old. The woman stayed upstairs with her dog that never came downstairs but somehow managed to leave the entire house reeking of his presence. The paper-thin walls were no buffer for the incessant tail thumping and yelping. We used a hot plate and microwave to cook our meals because the gas connection to the stove didn't work. The daughter didn't live there but loosely managed the property and cared for her mother. She made several appointments with the gas company to have the stove connected, but Freddy was irresponsible and never home to let the service guy in.

For four months, our diet consisted mostly of fast food. If it wasn't fast food, we ate whatever we could scavenge from the gas station convenience store. There isn't much that you can get at one of those places. The first time I tasted beef jerky, it was purchased at that same gas station convenience store with Freddy while we were out of town. I'm surprised I don't have high blood pressure because I must have eaten at least a hundred of those things while we were out there. There were the rare occasions we went to a restaurant in town to get a hamburger or a steak to go. I tried to discourage Freddy from spending so much money on food. This wasn't a vacation, we were grinding.

I was trying to help mold the youngster but passing the time during the day was one of the biggest challenges. Freddy never had cable installed at the place. There was a place about five minutes from where we stayed that sold old DVDs, so we stocked up. Freddy also made borrowing movies from customers one of his habits. When we went to serve them, there were a lot of times we ended up hanging out for a bit. Freddy had known most of his clientele since he was much younger, so chilling with them was no big deal. Most of the time, they were worried about getting high and paid no attention to us rummaging through their movie collections. After a while, Freddy began shopping for movies as soon as we walked in. When we found a good movie, it wasn't unheard of for us to watch the same movie four or five times straight. One time I remember that we got our hands on "The Lord of the Rings" trilogy which was the perfect nine hours of entertainment we needed. The customer we got it from wasn't stupid and the next time we went to her house, she definitely asked for her movie back. She was a heavy-set white woman in her mid-to-late thirties who was married to a black dude. There seemed to be a lot of interracial couples up there in the Berkshires. She always called me "Jesus" because she said, "I was so tall, it was as if I was up there with Jesus."

We almost always drank and smoked weed when we were watching movies, which I later found out wasn't a good idea. Freddy had a very low tolerance for both substances and instead of just going to sleep, he would become agitated and irrational. He had some real deep-rooted issues stemming from him being in foster care, and they only came to the surface when he was under the influence. There was one time he told me about him being a 7-year- old watching his older brothers "bag up work". Little Freddy, using salt, pretended to be doing the same. It's no wonder he grew up, following in their footsteps.

In addition to the lack of amenities and odors, there was no shower that I could use. The shower was a flimsy aftermarket stand up shower installed in the middle of a room after the house is already built. I didn't mind though; I was too big for it and the floor of the shower looked like it hadn't been cleaned in eons. There was no telling what type of fungus was growing on that floor, so I chose to take bird baths in the sink. We were only up there for five days at a time at the most; so, I figured I'd wait until I got back down to the city to take a proper shower. The sleeping arrangements posed a separate issue. Freddy had an air mattress to sleep on, but I had to fashion a bed out of an old loveseat and a chair that I used like an ottoman. I have slept in several weird places and positions in the past, so I was able to adjust easily, but the conditions were less than ideal. Had I been any other type of person, I wouldn't have been able handle being out of town. Looking back, while it may not have been easy, it wasn't anything that I wasn't built for. I would have went through much worse if it meant providing for my family.

Like most dudes that sell drugs out of town, Freddy had a local girl that he dated. That first weekend we went up there, he had me take him to her job and much to my surprise, she was a white girl. I looked at Freddy as just a regular cat from the hood, and def didn't think he was smooth enough to bag a white chick. Later, in retrospect, I realized I shouldn't have been surprised. The further into the countryside you travel, the fewer people of color you're likely to see.

In time, I saw Freddy was like most of us, and he had more than one side to him. While he was reckless and out of control at times, Freddy, also had a spiritually intelligent side as well. His girl bartended in a large wooden cabin which was the local hang out. The place looked like what I imagined any small mountain town hangout would look like. There was a bar, a few pool tables, and a fireplace. We went there to meet up with one of his customers. While we were waiting, I munched on a burger and fries while Freddy chatted to his girl, . At this point we were just hanging out, so after the burger I went over and shot a game of pool with his customer, Mike. There were three Mikes that Freddy served; this Mike, had the strangest snicker when he laughed. It was probably from the years of using, but he was cool though. I liked Mike.

Freddy sold crack. For a product he would get $20 for in the city he sold for $100 up in Massachusetts. Freddy was basically holding down the fort while his older brothers were locked up. Most of his customers came as a result of going up there with his brothers over the years. Initially, I stayed the first weekend and then drove Freddy back down to New York. Our arrangement was I would get $600 for the round trip, plus $100 for every day that I spent out of town. Additionally, Freddy would be responsible for all food and gas related expenses. The deal was sweet, but one could easily say it still wasn't worth it. So, I'll explain why I decided to take the chance with Freddy.

The first thing that had me interested was the fact that he worked alone. Tone and Kevin got caught up because they had too many people connected to them. When there are too many moving parts, anyone can be the one, to fuck things up. In their case, some idiot decided to get greedy and bring the heroin to town which led to kids OD'ing. A two-man operation, with us, meant I could keep an eye on and somewhat control what went on.

Another thing that helped sway my decision to work with Freddy was he had a very small circle of customers. Most of them had been handed down from his older brother so they looked at him like family. If he was dealing with strangers, I wouldn't have done it. New customers only came through one of his trusted custies. Without an intro, Freddy wasn't going to deal with them.

The third and most important reason was that Freddy was extra cautious, almost to the point of paranoia. We seldom were seen driving around during the daytime, with the only exception being if we were arriving or leaving town. Freddy never liked to drive through the middle of town, so he insisted on us traveling along a long series of back roads to avoid any police contact. After a while, I started to complain about all the indirect routes we were taking. "I'm not tryna get us locked up son, I'd rather be safe than sorry…," was his response. I respected it because I wasn't trying to get locked up either.

The fourth reason for my decision, and possibly the most important was, the money was great. In December of 2008, I stopped working with my cab base. At that point, most of my business came from regular customers calling my cell phone so I didn't need to pay the base for a service I hardly used. Prior to meeting Freddy, things had been a bit of a struggle for me. I saw working with him as a way to get money without having to work too hard. Out of town with Fred, my responsibilities were to sit around the house all day until around would 9 PM and make a few runs to serve his customers.

There were occasions when the phone would ring at three or four in the morning, and we would have to get up to make a run. The same thing happened to me when I was by myself in New York, so getting up in the middle of the night was no big deal. Freddy made calculated decisions; when we moved around, he carried small amounts of drugs on him. In the event of a bust, the charges I would have faced, if I faced any at all, would have been minimal.

The biggest chance we took came when we went to see another one of his customers named Mike, who we nicknamed "White Mike from Canaan." Canaan is in the neighboring state of Connecticut, so we had to cross state lines in order to serve him, which also meant additional charges if we were caught. Mike was a personable guy, about thirty at the time of us meeting, who stood about 5'8" with a pudgy body. He shared a modest home with his wife, mother-in-law, two kids and dogs. Additionally, his wife's brother was at their house all of the time. Despite the underlying foul odor from the dogs chilling at his house was always fun. They were some real backwoods country folks who were quite familiar with a few things that us city slickers had only heard about.

One day we were having a conversation about venison when his wife said, "I'm making a lasagna using venison tomorrow. Feel free to come by to pick some up." I had never eaten dear before. As you know, cooking at Freddy's crib wasn't an option, so I jumped at the chance to eat a home-cooked meal. Another night we were standing outside and getting ready to leave. Freddy was smoking a cigarette before he got in the truck when the brother-in-law was there and asked if Freddy had another cigarette. As soon as Freddy handed him the cigarette that he was keeping behind his ear, the brother-in-law said with a chuckle, "Did you nigga lick this cigarette?" Now I don't know what "nigga lick" means, it must be some country hick shit I don't know about. I do know, it's one thing when a Black person says, "nigga" and it's a completely different thing when it is coming from a non-black. In any event you can't let people and their ignorant comments take you out of your element. "What the fuck did you say?" asked Freddy angrily. This time, I understood Freddy's rage, but I had to intervene. "Yo! Aye yo! That's not cool, you can't say no shit like that to us..." I said forcefully. "Freddy, chill out, he don't know no better. Just be cool..." I said as I extended my arms out to form a wedge between him and the brother.

"Let's get the fuck out of here Rah," he said as he flicked his cigarette butt on the ground. "Fuckin idiot…" It was about 4 AM, and if a fight broke out there is a good chance it would have drawn the attention of the neighbors, who probably would have called the cops. We were two Black dudes in rural America, so when the cops came, there is no question which one of the two would be viewed as the aggressor. Also, Freddy had drugs on him, and didn't need any police contact.

The final reason which ultimately swayed my decision on working with Freddy was a simple one; I considered Tone a friend of mine, and I didn't want to see his little brother get locked up. Things had not worked out for him and my brother, but I didn't harbor any ill will and didn't want his brother to get caught up. In my opinion, all Freddy needed was a little guidance and he would be just fine.

As it turned out, working with Freddy wasn't as easy as I thought it would be. Freddy liked to try and control those around him. His go-to method was using money to influence decisions. Understandably, he grew used to the idea of having me around so much, that at times when I didn't want to stay up there, he tried to manipulate the situation in an effort to make me stay. One night we were at this guy Steve's house drinking and shooting pool with him and his wife. Freddy was trying to get me drunk so I would be too tired to drive back to New York. What he didn't know was that I used to be a heavy drinker and was capable of handling far more alcohol than the average person. Around 1:30 AM, I turned to Freddy and said, "I know you were trying to get me drunk so I'd stay, but I'm still leaving son." He laughed, "Ok, Rah. If you want to leave,

I can't stop you…" he reached in his pocket and handed me $800, "Here. Good looks."

    It was the first snowstorm of the season; the snowflakes were huge, and the roads were terrible. It was late, so the highways hadn't been plowed yet and there was only one set of tire tracks that all the cars were staying in. I was stuck behind an eighteen-wheel tractor trailer going about thirty miles per hour westbound on I-84. It was bad enough I was a little tired and tipsy, driving extra slow behind the truck was making it worse. Feeling myself getting sleepy, I called my friend, Shondell, to keep me company while I drove. We were on the phone for around twenty minutes when I began to get increasingly more frustrated. "Fuck this shit, I am going to pass him," "No, you're not Rah. Don't do it, you stay right where you are, He can see things that you can't" she fired back immediately. "Listen, I'm gonna call you back. I need both hands," I said as I hung up. I pulled to the into the left lane to pass him. As I tried to straighten the wheel again Candy began to fishtail. My front end was heading into the side of the truck. Knowing that's not a good idea, I jerked the wheel back the other direction……

To Be Continued in Volume 2

www.ingramcontent.com/pod-product-compliance
Lightning Source LLC
Chambersburg PA
CBHW060908120626
46553CB00001B/255